ATTITUDES
THAT ATTRACT
SUCCESS

You are only one attitude away
from a great life

WAYNE CORDEIRO

OMF LITERATURE INC.
Manila, Philippines

Cover design by Nixon Na
Page design by Aileen Barrongo

Published (2005) in the Philippines by
OMF Literature Inc.
776 Boni Avenue
Mandaluyong City, Metro Manila
www.OMFLit.com

Reprinted — 2005, 2006, 2007 (twice), 2008, 2009, 2010, 2011 (twice), 2012 (twice), 2013

ISBN 978-971-511-899-6

Printed in the Philippines

CONTENTS

Rarely have I seen anything that can be so powerful as a person's attitude. And rarely have I seen anything that can be so devastating.

For some, their attitude finds opportunity in every difficulty; others find difficulty in every opportunity. Some climb obstacles with a positive attitude, while others fall because of a negative outlook. Your attitude will either attract success or repel it.

Which of these tendencies describes you?

Before you answer that question, let me give you some good news: You can *choose* which it will be!

How is this possible? Because attitude is a *choice*. It is not a feeling, nor is it the result of an event or circumstances, good or bad. We are all individually responsible to build our view of life. The Bible says, "Whatever a man sows, this he will also reap" (Gal. 6:7). Our attitude toward life and our subsequent actions help determine what will happen to us. Our future looks bright when the attitude is right, and it makes the present much more enjoyable, too!

More than any other factor, the condition of your attitude will determine

- the quality of your relationships with other people;
- whether you can turn a problem into a blessing;
- whether you become a victim of defeat or a student of success.

The simple fact that attitude "makes" some while "breaking" others is a significant enough reason for us to explore how it works and how it is cultivated. The attitude we develop will cause us to see life either as a series of opportunities or in terms of our probabilities for failure. How a person defines life's events will do more than anything else to determine his or her potential for success in life. How true it is that you are one attitude away from a bright future!

But let me give to you, the reader, one important piece of advice. This is a book to be *applied*. You don't have to be gifted or exceptionally bright to employ these truths in your life, but *you must be willing!*

Before the following words can be transferred from ink on paper into permanent life change, you have to be convinced that a great attitude is one of the most important characteristics you can develop this year and every year! If you will approach this book in that way, the process of permanent change will be a joyful journey filled with adventure. It will change not only you but also every person with whom you come in contact.

Join me for the adventure.

John C. Maxwell
Founder, The INJOY Group

ACKNOWLEDGMENTS

I have had so many mentors over the years for whom I am eternally grateful—scores of people who have incredible spirits and attitudes of excellence. When observing these precious people, I would often find myself whispering, "Oh, God, make *me* like that, too."

My earliest memories are of my mother, who loved unreservedly. She stood only 4'11", but she will always be a giant in my heart. A single mom, she would constantly bolster my spirit with fresh hope through her songs and her encouragement.

Thank you to my wife, Anna, with whom I have chosen to share my life. She has been a stable pillar of support, full of compassion and a gracious spirit. Anna, you have taught me so much simply by being the person God made you to be.

Carol Ann Shima, you are the best encourager I have ever met. You always make people stand taller and walk more confidently after having been in your presence. Dan Shima, you are a solid fortress on the outside and a gracious servant and friend on the inside. I will always be grateful for the two of you.

Thank you to the many people who have modeled to me the heart of God.

I hesitate to begin thanking all those who have influenced me through the years, because it would fill far too many pages—and I fear I might still exclude more than I would remember. Allow me at least to say thank you to the wonderful people at New Hope Christian Fellowship. Every single one of you has touched my life, leaving an indelible mark of the Savior's fingerprints behind.

This book is for leaders, businesspeople, homemakers and young people. No matter what your background is or what your occupation may be, the principles of this book can transform your life and relationships. The only prerequisite is that you be an avid student of life.

Ralph Waldo Emerson once said, "The future belongs to those who prepare for it." This book will help you to do just that.

In my time as a pastor and leader, I have watched people, studied them and observed what makes one successful and another not. I have seen talented, educated and skilled people fail. On the other hand, I have witnessed the success of those who possess very little talent, education or skill.

Many people are not that far from a life of joy and success. Just a few adjustments and life would come in loud and clear for them! Like a radio that's not tuned quite right, the music can be heard but it's full of static and fades in and out. A small turn of the dial would recalibrate the frequency by just a few hertz. Then, all of a sudden, voila! The scratchy signal is transformed into a stereophonic symphony of sound!

Your attitude is where that small adjustment must be made. Attitude can mean the difference between success and failure. Someone once said the difference between people is very small, but that very small difference is very big indeed!

Living a life of joy and success is something God has already wired into your design. Did you know that? He has planned your future to be one of success. God takes no joy or glory in a mediocre life. Fruitfulness is what God wants for each of us, and He's ready to help us achieve it!

You did not choose Me, but I chose you, and appointed you, that you should go and bear fruit, and that your fruit should remain, that whatever you ask of the Father in My name, He may give to you (John 15:16).

Let God help you to develop an attitude that attracts success. He's poised to do so. Cooperate with Him. Apply the principles of this book, and you will be well on your way to fruitfulness!

BECOME A STUDENT OF LIFE

I love to watch people, especially successful people—people who are successful in business, relationships and finances. And I have learned there is a reason they're successful. Success doesn't happen by accident; people don't stumble onto it by mistake. There are solid reasons why these men and women are successful, and they leave clues behind for us to observe and collect—if we will look for them. A willing student of life will examine these clues and learn that anyone can develop an attitude that attracts success!

One of my favorite pastimes while attending college in Portland, Oregon, involved going to the airport and finding a nice bench adjacent to one of the main thoroughfares. I would take a seat and, for an hour or two, I would watch people.

I know what you may be thinking, that I am a bit off-kilter. Maybe you're right. Nevertheless, that's what I did. Before you write me off, however, stay with me a moment longer.

I would see a businessman hurrying on his way to an important appointment. I would observe how he was dressed, his mannerisms, the speed with which he walked, the way he would converse with others around him, and I would evaluate his countenance. Did he carry on his face a look of anxiety, joy, despair or concern?

Then I would spot a young mother carrying a child from one terminal to another, and I would try to discern what kind of a person she was. Was she secure or fearful? What kind of day was she having? Was she successful? Was there peace in her heart or was there worry?

I watched students, workers, airport officials and others as they walked to and fro in the concourse. I observed the way they stood, sat, walked and communicated with one another. I watched the focus of their eyes when in conversation. I observed how they would greet friends or family members who had come to pick them up. And I pondered what it was that made one person successful and another not. What made one life happy and filled with joy, while another seemed empty and hollow?

Each of those lives had a story behind it—a story of struggle or success, of abandon or hope, of pessimism or promise.

Through the years, I have collected and catalogued scores of observations of failure and success. I have attempted to distill the principles I learned and record them for other students of life, like yourself.

Never stop learning. Make it a lifelong goal. Discover new truths and insights that will awaken your spirit. New horizons will help you to always look ahead and focus on your potential rather than on your problems, on your future rather than on your failures.

SHARE IN THE FELLOWSHIP OF THE WHITE BELT

I remember reading about Jigoro Kano, the founder of the martial art of judo. Kano's story is a lesson of inspiration and motivation for every student of life.

Kano possessed an extraordinary willingness to learn. He sought out the nearly defunct martial art of jujitsu and modified it to incorporate modern sports principles, creating the art of judo. It became the defense system of the Japanese police and was the first Eastern martial art to be accepted in international competition at the Olympics.

Kano was so focused on learning improved techniques in all walks of life that he found new and better ways for the island nation of Japan to educate its youth. He became known as the father of modern Japanese education. Kano was well respected in athletic, social and political circles worldwide.

Just before he died, this world-renowned martial arts expert called his students together. As they congregated to hear the final words of their judo master, he announced, "When you bury me, do not bury me in a black belt! Be sure to bury me in a white belt!"

In martial arts the white belt is the symbol of a beginner—an apprentice who has many things yet to learn.

What a lesson in humility and teachability! Each of us, regardless of our ranking in life, must become a lifelong learner. Whether you are a CEO, a pastor, a secretary, a parent, a child, a leader or follower—under all of your roles, always wear a white belt.

Even if you are an expert in your field, continue to value learning. By continuing to learn, you will continue to be an expert. As soon as we stop learning, we will begin to stiffen and atrophy!

LEARN FROM THE PROFILES OF TWO HEROES

People often ask me who my heroes are. One is Wendy Stoker.

Wendy attended a Midwest high school and, in her final year, finished just 3.5 points behind first place in girls' diving. She went to an East Coast college, where she took a full load of classes, was on the bowling team, participated in student government and continued her diving. But what I find most spectacular about this young woman is her typing skill. As a college freshman she typed at a "whizzing"—well, sort of—40 words per minute.

Did I forget to mention that Wendy Stoker was born without arms?

She types 40 words per minute with her toes.

What is it that causes a person to possess such determination, such courage, such an indomitable spirit? Before I discuss that, let me share with you about another of my heroes.

Thomas Alva Edison invented the incandescent lightbulb, the movie camera and the batteries that start our cars. Toward the autumn years of his life, he worked in a modest building that resembled a barn. There, with his son, Edison would often remain late into the night, laboring to perfect his inventions. One evening, in an attempt to improve the retention of a battery's charge, an unfortunate combination of chemicals caused his latest experiment to burst into flames. The fire quickly spread through the old wooden structure, and what began as a minor chemical combustion exploded into a towering inferno.

Edison's son quickly evacuated the building. Using his smock to shield him from the heat of the flames, he desperately called for his father, fearing Edison might still be in the barn trying to save his precious lifework. Running frantically, the young man circled the barn, hoping his father had escaped through another exit. On his second time around the building, he turned a corner and, to his great relief, there stood his legendary father. Edison's hands were buried deep in his soot-speckled smock, his white hair blackened with ash. He was watching intently as flames devoured the structure.

"Father!" cried Edison's son. "I was afraid you were still inside!"

Without taking his eyes off the flames, Edison said, with a sense of urgency, "Son, go get your mother!"

"Why, Dad?"

With a twinkle in his eyes his father replied, "Because your mother comes from a small town and she's never seen a fire like this before!"

When the flames had finished their work, leaving only ash and a twisted frame, Edison turned to his son. "You know anyone who has a tractor?"

"Yes, Dad, but why?"

Edison answered, "Because it's time to rebuild, Boy. It's time to rebuild."

Wendy Stoker and Thomas Edison. What great models for each of us! But what was it that kept them going, though the odds were stacked against them? What was the fuel that compelled them to move beyond their setbacks?

In heroes well known or unsung, you'll find one common thread, one common denominator. In every case, it is attitude! That's right. Attitude.

PEOPLE WHO ARE EFFECTIVE HAVE USED SETBACKS AS STEPPING-STONES; WHEREAS INEFFECTIVE PEOPLE HAVE USED THEM AS EXCUSES.

Your attitude is more important than you will ever realize. It's the most important thing about you—more important than your education, your past, your looks or your money. Your attitude will help you make friends or cause you to make enemies. It will attract people to you or repel them.

Your attitude is even more important than your skills in determining your ability to succeed. John D. Rockefeller once said, "I will pay a man more for his attitude and his ability to get along with others than for any other skill he may possess." Your attitude is one of your most important assets.

What is important is not the current state of your family, your problems, who your boss is or how much money you make.

What *is* important is your *attitude* toward family, toward problems, toward authority and toward money. Attitude makes all the difference in the world! You'll find that both effective and ineffective people have experienced setbacks. However, the people who are effective have used those setbacks as stepping-stones, whereas ineffective people have used them as excuses.

I am absolutely convinced of the truth behind the maxim, "Ten percent of life is made up of what happens to you—the other 90 percent is how you *respond* to what happens to you." That's where character is built. That's where personality is formed. That's where attitude is expressed.

Find two people who attended the same schools, had the same teachers, shop at the same stores, live in the same city and even attend the same church. One struggles and the other is successful. Why?

Attitude.

A Fragrance or a Bad Odor?
The Choice Is Yours

In Hawaii, we have a custom of giving leis to one another as an act of hospitality, honor or friendship. A lei is usually made up of flowers strung together and draped around a person's neck. We give leis to say, "Thank you," and we give leis to say, "Goodbye."

I love the fragrant flowers of Hawaii. The pikake, the plumeria, the white ginger and the *pua kenikeni* are my favorites. These beautiful flowers are so pungent that everywhere I turn, the wafting fragrance adds a sense of Polynesian aloha to everything I experience. When I wear one of these leis, every person I meet smells wonderful! It does not matter whether the person is tall or short, happy or sad, coming to me with a complaint or a compliment, they all smell wonderful to me! Of course, this fragrance I enjoy has nothing to do with the person I am with but has everything to do with the lei I am wearing.

Attitude is like a lei. Each of us has one, but we have made a choice of what to string together to make up that lei. If you carry around a collection of dried fish, everything starts to smell fishy. If you string together old socks, the whole world seems to have this funny odor to it. Your attitude is like a fragrance you carry around with you. The difference is that skunks carry around a *bad odor*, while the beautiful Hawaiian plumeria blossoms carry a *fragrance*.

Whether you like it or not, each of us carries either a fragrance or a bad odor. You choose which you will carry. Some people's poor attitudes follow them around like bad cologne. Others who have wonderful personalities leave a fragrance in their wake as they pass through our lives.

YOUR ATTITUDE AFFECTS YOUR HEALTH

When you are stressed or worried, your body secretes a powerful hormone called adrenaline. The effects of adrenaline in the human body can be compared to those of rocket fuel in a missile or nitric oxide in a race car. Adrenaline is shot into your blood to give you an immediate boost of energy or strength in response to fear, excitement or extreme emotion. In other words, it gives you an energy blast to get you going *fast*.

Once when I was jogging, I passed a fenced yard that was the domain of two massive Doberman pinschers. I didn't see the dogs—"flesh-eating canines" would be a more accurate term—as I jogged past the yard. I guess they felt I was jogging too close to their boundary line, so out of nowhere, they charged me, with vicious, blood-curdling barking. Out of the corner of my eye, I caught sight of the two demonic figures fiercely bearing down on me. Adrenaline shot through my body like a bullet through soft cheese. At the time of the attack, it never occurred to me there was a protective fence separating their ugly teeth from my pristine body. So I jumped three feet straight into the air and darted off faster than I had run since high school.

Adrenaline is a powerful chemical designed to be burned up immediately by the body. If it is not expended, however, it can affect you adversely. Your body doesn't know whether it is being attacked from without or within. Likewise, a critical attitude puts your body on an all-points alert, and your internal systems go on the defensive. If I carry around a critical attitude, for example, small doses of adrenaline drip into my bloodstream all day long. With the presence of adrenaline in our system, we get irritable, we may be cynical, we age faster, we hurt, and even with eight hours of sleep, we may still be tired when we awake.

Medical researchers tell us that stress and worry cause more internal damage than we realize. Physiologically, we are affected by fear, insecurity and unresolved bitterness. These things weaken our immune system, causing us to become susceptible to viruses and diseases our bodies would normally be capable of fending off.

A dear friend of mine was once the picture of health. He ate only the best foods, exercised and monitored his cholesterol levels vigilantly. But he had one major malady—worry. He worried about anything he could not completely control, until it ate him up inside. He had a tough time trusting God for his future, his finances and his family. As his anxiety grew, so did the physical effects. He constantly fell victim to stomach ailments.

He appeared to be in his 60s even though he was only 52. I also watched him go through a second divorce—the stress had cost him another loving relationship.

This dear friend recently passed away at an early age. Although he was a health nut, he succumbed to something much more devastating: a terrible perspective on life. His attitude had stolen his best years.

I have heard it said that the presence of adrenaline in your blood system can increase your cholesterol count by 40 percent. We willingly go on exotic diets and take pills to reduce our cholesterol level, when what we really need is a better attitude toward life!

You could say that the state of your health is determined not so much by what you're eating but by *what's eating you.*

IS YOUR ATTITUDE BROKEN?

A man made an appointment to see his doctor. "Doctor," he complained, "everywhere I touch seems to hurt lately. Am I getting old or just senile? If I push on my knees here, I hurt. I push on my stomach and I hurt! I press on my head right here by my temple and that hurts, too! What's going on?"

The doctor called for a full body X ray.

An hour passed and after evaluating the X rays carefully, the doctor returned. Stroking his chin, the doctor slowly began, "I think I've found the reason why everything you touch hurts."

"Well, tell me!" the man anxiously replied.

The doctor pointed to the X ray. "Your body is fine, but your finger is broken."

Our attitude is like that finger. If our attitude stinks, everything around us stinks. If our attitude is good, everything will seem fragrant!

How is your attitude? Is it like a bad odor that follows you around? Or is it a beautiful fragrance that makes any situation more pleasant? Take some time right now to evaluate yourself before you read on.

Evaluating My Attitude

1 Am I a lifelong learner? Or have I allowed my position in life to determine that I no longer need to learn?
   a. Do I value learning?
   b. Am I teachable? Humble?

2 What is my attitude toward problems, authority, family and money?
   a. How are my personal relationships with family, friends, coworkers and neighbors?
   b. If others were to rank my personality, would they say that I leave a bad odor in my wake or do I leave a beautiful fragrance for others to enjoy?

3 Generally, how do I respond to what happens to me? With worry or calm? With a good attitude or a bad attitude?
   a. Do I view setbacks as stepping-stones or excuses?
   b. How do I react when the odds are against me?
   c. How would I rate myself in stress/worry?
   d. Do I suffer from ailments (e.g., stomach upset, headaches, tiredness or broken relationships) that indicate critical attitude, stress or worry?

CHAPTER ONE

MAKE YOUR CHOICE

Blessed are the poor in spirit, for theirs is the kingdom of heaven.

Blessed are the gentle, for they shall inherit the earth.

Blessed are the merciful, for they shall receive mercy.

Blessed are the pure in heart, for they shall see God.

Blessed are the peacemakers, for they shall be called sons of God.

MATTHEW 5:3,5,7–9

The Sermon on the Mount—perhaps Jesus' most famous sermon—addresses our attitudes. Theologians have called this series of teachings the Beatitudes. I guess His lesson could be summed up this way: "Your attitudes will determine what you will be." Hence, the Be-attitudes.

Jesus knew that developing a correct perspective on life was critically important to our lives and to our ministries, and so He spoke first and often on that very topic. In fact, before Jesus taught His disciples about miracles, discipleship or how to deal with the Pharisees, He taught them about attitudes! Every phrase of the Beatitude deals with building right attitudes because they become the lamp of the body (see Matt. 6:22-23), the very way we see and interpret the world around us.

An interesting scientific theorem states that if your basic premise is inaccurate, then every subsequent conclusion thereafter will also be inaccurate. What this means is that if you are solving a math problem and you begin by determining $2 + 2 = 5$, then all of your following calculations will be incorrect. Likewise, if my core attitudes and perspectives toward life and people are skewed, then I too will experience massacre after massacre in the form of devastated relationships, foiled expectations and broken dreams.

Jesus knew that from the core of our beings, we need to develop a right attitude toward life. Let your eye, your attitude, be clear and your every conclusion thereafter will have the potential for success!

A POOR ATTITUDE CAN COST YOU

The president of the Bank of America told the following story, which took place some years ago.

The Los Angeles branch of the Bank of America is housed in a multilevel building with a parking structure on its lower floors. This large skyscraper housed many businesses. For many years, customers using the bank would not be charged for parking if they simply presented a ticket to the teller for validation with any transaction.

Over the years, however, people began abusing this privilege by making small or insignificant transactions at the bank and then spending the rest of the day shopping at other businesses in the building. Due to the frequent infractions by shrewd customers, the bank reluctantly discontinued the privilege of validating tickets for free and unlimited parking. Validated tickets would henceforth be charged at a discounted hourly rate.

One morning, an elderly man dressed in jeans and a flannel shirt waited his turn in a long line of customers. The line slowly inched its way forward, until he made his way to the next open teller's booth. The man made a small deposit and presented his parking ticket for validation. The teller stamped his ticket and informed him that he would have to pay a small amount for the parking.

"Why? You've never required this before," the elderly customer replied.

The teller, faced with a crowded bank full of impatient customers, snapped, "Well that's the new rule. I don't make 'em. I just dish 'em out."

"But I've been a customer in this bank for many years," the man persisted. "The least you can do is validate it like you used to."

"You heard me, Mister. You got a problem with that, see the manager. I have a lot of people waiting behind you. If you could move along, that would make this morning go by a little easier."

The flannel-shirted gentleman made his way to the end of the long line of waiting customers, and once again he inched his way back toward the tellers' booths. When he finally arrived, he approached the first available teller, withdrew $4.2 million and went across the street and deposited it in another bank.

That teller's attitude cost the bank $4.2 million! Never underestimate the destruction that can be wrought by a poor attitude.

A sign hanging on the wall of an old gas station holds for us a poignant truth. It reads:

Why Customers Quit
1% die.
3% move.
5% leave because of location.
7% quit because of product dissatisfaction.
84% of customers quit because of an attitude of
     indifference shown to them by one of the employees!

CHOOSE LIFE

I call heaven and earth to witness against you today, that I have set before you life and death, the blessing and the curse. So choose life in order that you may live (Deut. 30:19).

God tells us that the choice between life and death, between a blessing or a curse is up to us! He almost pleads with His people, telling us to choose *life* in order that we may live. God not only gives us a choice, He goes further and tells us what choice we should make. He even shows us the benefits of making the right choice, and He lets us know the consequences should we choose otherwise.

In essence, God is saying, "Here's your choice, life or death, a fruitful future or one of pain. But wait! Before you choose, let Me tell you which is best. Choose life that you may live, both you and your descendants. Got it? Okay, now choose."

Do you remember "Let's Make a Deal"? On this 1970s TV game show, would-be contestants in the studio audience would dress up like squirrels, ducks, redwoods and various household appliances and act nuts to get the attention of the show's host, Monty Hall. On one of the shows, Monty pointed to a housewife dressed as a chicken and said, "Chicken, come on down!"

IF YOU KNOW THESE THINGS, YOU ARE BLESSED IF YOU DO THEM.

JOHN 13:17, EMPHASIS ADDED

The lady pecked her way toward the aisle, jumping up and down excitedly and molting all over the host. Monty then pointed out three large doors on the stage and said, "You can have whatever is behind door number one, door number two or door number three. Which one are you going to choose?" The helpful studio audience yelled out, "One!" "No, pick two!" "Three! Three! Pick three!" all at the same time.

The chicken made her choice: "Three!"

Monty then said, "Before I show you what's behind door number three, let me show you what's behind door number one!" The door was opened and there stood a pair of Mercedes Benz luxury automobiles.

Wails of sorrow rose from the chicken and from the audience.

Monty continued, "Now let me show you what's behind door number two!" The door opened and a voice announced, "A 50-foot sailboat and a vacation in Acapulco!"

More groans of disappointment.

"And now," Monty said, "let me show you what you have chosen behind door number three!" The door opened to reveal a donkey.

The chicken lady threw her hands up in despair, as the audience echoed her woe over such a poor choice. Wasn't that tragic?

Now let me share with you something even more tragic. Imagine if the game show had gone like this:

Monty says, "You can have whatever is behind door number one, door number two or door number three. Which door will you choose? But wait! Before you tell us, let me show you what's behind every door! Behind door number one are two luxury cars! Behind door number two we have a sailboat and a vacation in Acapulco! Behind door number three is a donkey. Got it?"

"Uh, okay!" the chicken lady replies, and the crowd goes wild in anticipation.

"Now, which one will you choose? Door number one, door number two or door number three?"

She pauses for a second, listening to the confusing barnyard calls of the other animals in the studio audience.

"Oh . . . uh . . . well . . . ," she nervously deliberates. "Door number three!"

Now *that* would be tragic!

Nevertheless, as dumb as it sounds, that's exactly what we do. So often God shows us the consequences of making a bad choice or walking through life with a bad attitude, and yet we choose that attitude anyway. Then when relationships fail, when we lose friends or forfeit a great opportunity, it really should be no surprise.

"Have this attitude in yourselves which was also in Christ Jesus" (Phil. 2:5). Take time with me over these next chapters to deposit into your heart the necessary ingredients to develop a life-changing attitude. Make that choice right now. It may come slowly at first, but don't give up. The new attitude may feel awkward at first, but practice until it becomes natural.

You are only one attitude away from a great life, a successful marriage and a promising future!

CHAPTER TWO

BELIEVE YOU CAN CHANGE

According to your faith will it be done to you.

MATTHEW 9:29, *NIV*

No one has been given an unalterable attitude. You *can* change, but it's up to you. Decide now how you want to approach life and develop that kind of attitude. A new attitude doesn't happen on its own. You must develop it, and the sooner you begin, the better.

Some people hide behind the excuse that they just can't change: "I've been this way since I was a kid, and I'm not about to change now." It's never too late to change! Change is indispensable to growth. If you stop changing, you stop growing. And if you stop growing, you're in trouble! What do you call a tree that has stopped growing? That's right. *Dead*. It's no different with people. When they stop growing, they start dying.

Some people stopped growing years ago. We might not bury them until they have stopped moving, but they really died years ago.

You *can* change your attitude.

Thank goodness for one church secretary who was willing to change hers. One morning, a big Texan wearing a 10-gallon hat sauntered into the church office and sidled up to the counter. "I came in to talk with the head pig of this church," he confidently drawled with a heavy accent.

"The head . . . *what?*!" the shocked secretary replied.

"The head pig. Ya know, the one who blabs on and on every Sunday morning. Just wanted to talk with him before I head back to the ranch," the Texan continued, drawing out each syllable along the way.

Aghast at his irreverence, the prim and proper secretary straightened herself in her chair. With a voice resembling that of a grade-school teacher reprimanding a student, she retorted, "Now listen here. We don't use such terms of disrespect in this office. We call him 'Reverend' or 'Pastor,' but never anything less!"

"Well," the man drawled, "I never meant no disrespect, ma'am. I just sold a bunch of my stock and heard the good Lord tell me to donate a million dollars. Thought I'd like to do that here."

With a new sparkle in her voice, she quickly responded, "Wait right there. I'll go get the hog!"

A famous inventor said, "The world hates change, yet it is the only thing that has brought progress." How open to change are you? When we refuse to change and resist God's leading, life can become pretty miserable! Nevertheless, many times we won't change until the pain of remaining the same becomes greater than the pain of changing.

WHAT WILL NAVIGATE YOUR LIFE?

Before technology changed the way we navigate on the water, bullhorns and whistles were used to communicate from ship to ship. Once, a large armored battleship was slowly making its way through uncharted waters in a fog-shrouded bay.

Suddenly, through the fog, the captain noticed what appeared to be the light of another ship directly in his path. Quickly, he grabbed his megaphone and shouted, "This is Admiral Smith of the United States Navy. Steer yourself 10 degrees south. We are on a collision course, and I am coming through with priority orders."

Through the fog, he heard a faint but audible reply, "This is Seaman Fourth Class Jones. You steer *yourself* 10 degrees to the *north.*"

The Admiral said to himself, *This guy is a seaman fourth class, and I'm an admiral! Who in the world does he think he is?* Turning up the megaphone a few notches and using a stronger tone of authority, he barked, "This is Admiral Smith of the United States Navy! You steer your vessel 10 degrees south! I am coming through!"

Through the fog came the same reply. "This is Seaman Fourth Class Jones. You steer *yourself* 10 degrees *north*."

The admiral's anger flared at the young man's insubordination. "I said this is Admiral Smith. Steer yourself 10 degrees south immediately. I am a battleship!"

Through the fog, the unwavering voice replied, "This is Seaman Fourth Class Jones. Steer yourself 10 degrees north. *I am a lighthouse!*"

Our attitudes are like the rudder of a ship. You will either be ruled by the rudder, or you will be ruled by the rocks.

The choice is yours.

It Is an Issue of Faith

If we refuse to change, we're in trouble. If we think we can't change, we won't have the faith to change, even if it is possible. Jesus said, "According to your faith will it be done to you" (Matt. 9:29, *NIV*). If I don't have the faith that I can change or that my situation can change, then it won't.

On the other hand, if I believe I can change—*I can follow Jesus, I can do better in my marriage, God can use me*—then the Lord can say, "Now you've got the faith." A good attitude releases the Lord to do His work. If I say I can't, then I won't have the faith to cooperate with God's attempts to bring wholeness and healing to my life. My poor attitude will actually sabotage God's work in me.

Do you believe your marriage can change? You *must* believe it can. You must believe that your heart can change, that your family situation can change. God is able. The question is this: Are you willing?

In the Bible, God often commends or reprimands people based on the level of their faith. In Luke 8, a woman who had been ill for many years believed she would be healed if she could only touch the fringe of Jesus' cloak. When she did, Jesus said to her, "Your faith has made you well" (v. 48).

> ## "WE . . . ARE BEING TRANSFORMED INTO HIS LIKENESS WITH EVER-INCREASING GLORY, WHICH COMES FROM THE LORD, WHO IS THE SPIRIT."
>
> 2 CORINTHIANS 3:18, *NIV*

Do you have faith that you can change? You must believe you can be made well, that you can develop an attitude that attracts success. If you don't think you can, you won't. The choice is yours.

NO ONE TOLD HIM IT COULDN'T BE DONE

Everybody in this Southern California college knew that whoever achieved the best grade on the upcoming final exam would be offered the one and only position as the next assistant math professor.

George Dansig wanted the job so badly he couldn't sleep at night. His lifelong dream was to become a math professor, and this was his golden opportunity! Nothing must stand in his way. He was determined to correctly answer every question on the test. On the day of the final, George was still studying so intently that when he glanced at his watch, he realized he was 15 minutes late for the test! He quickly collected his books; then he ran to class and into the room. George tried to apologize for his tardiness, but the professor whispered, "Shhh," gave George the test papers and motioned for him to get started.

The test was more difficult than George had expected, but he was driven and completed all the questions. Just as he was about to turn his test in, however, George noticed two more problems written on the chalkboard. Figuring these were for extra credit, he turned his paper over and began working on them.

An excruciating battle of mind over math began, but his efforts would not be in vain. The invisible guardian over the science of math seemed to recognize his efforts and allowed him to answer the first query.

He tackled the second problem with the zeal of a trained athlete but soon knew he had met his match. Beads of sweat began to form on his brow. George was certain that if he didn't solve this final problem, someone else would! And he would be denied the one and only position of his dreams.

Just then, the professor called, "Time's up!" Dejected, George slumped in his seat like a defeated game-show contestant.

That night he couldn't sleep. He tossed and turned, fearing the worst. The next morning, George almost had to force himself to return to the class, where he would likely hear someone else's name announced as the new assistant math professor.

As he slowly entered the room, the professor stood up behind his desk and said, "Mr. George Dansig! You have made mathematical history!"

"I don't understand, sir."

The professor replied, "You were late yesterday, weren't you, George?"

"Yes, sir. I'm sorry. I was studying."

"No, no! Let me explain," he continued. "You see, George, this was going to be a hard test. So I warned the students before the final began that mathematics presents us with some very, very difficult problems and that this test would be no exception. In fact, there are some problems so difficult, we call them 'unsolvable problems.' As an example, I wrote two of them on the board—and you solved one of them!"

Let me ask you this: If George had been told he couldn't solve the problem, that it was impossible, do you think he would have even tried? Absolutely not!

Believe that you can change, and you will.

YOU GOTTA BELIEVE!

One man says, "I can." Another says, "I cannot." Which man is correct? Both. The Bible says, "For as [a man] thinks within himself, so he is" (Prov. 23:7).

The story is told of a Scotsman who was an extremely hard worker. He not only held himself to a high standard but set the same for those who were under him. During one project where

IF GOD HAS SAID THAT HE HAS A GREAT PLAN FOR YOUR LIFE, ISN'T IT TIME YOU BELIEVED HIM?

he was setting seemingly impossible deadlines for his men, a coworker needled him, saying, "Hey, Scotty! Don't you know that Rome wasn't built in a day?"

"Yes, I read about that," the Scotsman replied. "That's because I wasn't the foreman on that job!"

Do you accept the normal limitations that stop everyone else? Are you willing to accept what others accept? Don't do it! That's the beginning of mediocrity.

Remember the bumblebee. According to the known laws of aerodynamics, it should be scientifically impossible for the bumblebee to fly. The size, weight and shape of the bee's body in relation to its wingspan make it theoretically unable to get off the ground. But no one told the bumblebee, so it flies anyway, whatever the scientists might say!

"For I know the plans that I have for you," declares the LORD, "plans for welfare and not for calamity to give you a future and a hope" (Jer. 29:11).

If God has a great plan for our lives, isn't it time we believed the same? Isn't it time we believed what God believes? That's called faith, and our attitude is a direct barometer of our faith.

When the great architect Frank Lloyd Wright was 83 years old, he was asked which of his works would be remembered as his greatest masterpiece. He replied, "My next one!"

The future is brighter when your attitude is right. You'll have more energy, your creativity level will increase, and you'll stay younger!

WHERE'S THE STORM?

It has been said that the smallest of boats is safe in the roughest of seas, just as long as none of that rough sea gets inside that small boat! Developing an attitude that attracts success is an inside job. You see, having a godly attitude does not mean you will never face problems or storms.

I can't remember who wrote it, but an old poem I came across went something like this:

One ship sails east
and another sails west,
While the selfsame
breezes blow.
But it's the set of the sail
and not the winds
That determines
where it will go.
And as the storms rage on,
as we journey through life,
It will be the set of our hearts
that determines where we go,
Not the storms or strife.

Your attitude is the set of your sail. You must choose the direction you want your life to travel and set your heart accordingly. There will be storms, but it will be your attitude toward those storms that drives you in one direction or another, not the storm itself.

Each of us will be surrounded with problems at times, and we will often find ourselves steeped in hot water. But remember that the event will soon pass. The event is temporary, but the effects of how we respond in the midst of the event will last much longer. A poor attitude in the midst of the storm can cause the storm to rage inside for a lifetime.

NEVER LET OUTSIDE STORMS BECOME INSIDE STORMS

We will always face storms in life, but remember: Never allow an outside storm to become an inside storm.

It's inside storms that sink ships.

The Bible is replete with story after story of how God's people encountered problems.

When Noah sailed the ocean blue,
He had problems the same as you.
For 40 days he drove the ark,
Before he found a place to park.

How many times have we found ourselves flooded with problems? Often, when I have been surrounded with struggles in the ministry, I have felt like the lion tamer who put an ad in the paper: "Lion tamer—wants tamer lion."

A few years ago, I took up fishing as a hobby. Friends and I would fish on the eastern shore of the Big Island of Hawaii. We would throw our lines into the ocean, and if we were fishing at the right time and had the right bait, we would catch some good-sized fish. Nearby was a barbecue grill where we would place our trophies. We would take our day's catch, clean each one and then place each trophy on the grill. Even though these fish had spent all their lives in the salty ocean, guess what I had to sprinkle on our catch as we were cooking them? Right! I would sprinkle salt on the fish to bring out the flavor.

You would think that would be about the most unnecessary thing to do, considering that the fish had been marinating in saltwater for at least a year or two. Yet even though these fish had lived in the ocean, none of the salt got inside.

My point? If God can do that for fish, He can do that for each of us.

Each of us has been placed in the middle of a world filled with worldly perspectives and philosophies. But here's the wonder of God's design: Although we live in the midst of a "crooked and perverse generation" (Phil. 2:15), none of that crooked perverseness is supposed to get inside of us!

Your attitude will either protect you or defeat you in the midst of storms. Develop your attitude well.

SEE NEGATIVE CIRCUMSTANCES AS CHANGING

A few people have said to me, "I understand what you're saying about looking for what's right. But you can't deny that there are problems! There *will* *always* *be* problems. How do you deal with them practically?"

Sure, there will be problems, and each problem needs to be addressed. You need to meet them head on and courageously deal with them in a way that honors God and builds biblical character. However, here's a secret that has helped me over the years: Whenever you speak of problems, always speak of them as *changing*.

Someone says, "You have a problem." Your response should be, "Yes, I do, but it's changing!" Someone else says, "Well, you've got financial problems." Your answer? "Yes, but that's changing!" When someone says to you, "Hey, you have a bad marriage." You say, "Yeah, but it's changing!" When someone says "You've got bad breath," you can reply, "Yeah, but it's changing!"

When you speak of problems as changing, you see a hopeful light at the end of the darkened tunnel. This is a positive indicator that you are growing.

However, if someone says, "You've got financial problems," and you say, "Man, do I ever have financial problems! I have always *had* financial problems, and I will probably *always* *have* financial problems until Jesus comes," this attitude acts as a magnet, inviting depression and cynicism. It shuts down your creative problem-solving ability and causes you to freeze up, leaving you perpetually in this state of financial need.

You will see problems everywhere, but don't allow your eyes to remain focused on them. Look for answers and *that's* what you will see. Develop a new perspective—a fresh view of your problems. Solve them; don't dwell on them. You'll be tempted to remain in a slough of despair. It feels good, sometimes, to be pitied, and many of us look for reasons to remain in our unhappy circumstances. But don't do it.

Failure is not when you get knocked down. Failure is when you refuse to get back up. Don't hang around the swamps of despair. They will only skew your attitude and impede your resilience. Learn to bounce back quickly.

Someone once said to me, "When you go through hell, don't stop to take pictures."

I agree!

CHAPTER THREE

TRAIN YOUR EYES TO SEE WHAT IS GOOD

He who diligently seeks good seeks favor,

but he who searches after evil, it will come to him.

PROVERBS 11:27

All our lives, we have trained our eyes to see what is bad. From an early age, we have been training ourselves incorrectly. We get up and read the morning newspaper over breakfast, getting our minimum daily requirement of bad news. On the way to work, we stop by a newsstand and buy the latest issue of *U.S. Bad News and World Report*, so we can find out what's wrong with the world. After work we rush home and watch the "CBS Evening Bad News," then stay up late to watch the day's worst events all over again on the local 10 o'clock bad news. We then lay down for a restless night's sleep with bad dreams, only to get up with a bad attitude so we can have another bad day at work—just as we have done every day for years!

Train your eyes to see evidence of His presence, not evidence of His absence.

We have to retrain our eyes. The reason is this: *Whatever we're looking for is what we will see.* That's how God made us. If we are looking for something good, we will see what is good. If we're always looking for what's wrong with people, what will we see everywhere we turn? Everything that's wrong.

In 1984 we moved to a quiet little town called Hilo on the southernmost island in Hawaii. One day my wife came home and announced, "Honey, I know what I want!"

"What?" I asked.

"I want a Mazda MPV van. Buy me one!" she pleaded.

"Uh-uh," I grunted.

She said, "But it's a beautiful van!"

I had never seen a Mazda van. "Mazda doesn't make vans. I've never seen one."

She said, "Oh, yes! They make them. They're beautiful!"

"Honey, Mazda doesn't make vans."

She said, "Yes they do! Jump in the car!"

We climbed into the car and trekked into town. Within 15 minutes, a Mazda van pulled through an intersection we were approaching. My wife exclaimed, "There's one!"

I said, "That *is* nice! I didn't realize Mazda made vans."

Within 15 minutes, another one came by. She said, "There's another one! And that's the color I want! If you love me . . ."

Within the hour, we had seen six Mazda vans! I hadn't even known there was such a vehicle, but suddenly they were everywhere! Isn't that how it always works? When you're thinking of purchasing a certain car, you notice it everywhere. Everyone's driving your car!

Likewise, if we look for the best in other people, then we will see the most beautiful people in the world everywhere we turn.

What you are looking for, you will begin to see.

LOOK FOR EVIDENCE OF HIS PRESENCE

Train your eyes to see evidence of God's presence, not evidence of His absence. If you are looking for God's absence, you will conclude that this world is a God-forsaken place! On the other hand, if you are looking for evidence of His presence, you will soon see that He is with us even in the darkest of moments.

Sometimes we have a mistaken notion of spirituality. When stricken by this disease, once-stalwart Christians become pharisaical at best. This malady can infect any believer, but it more often strikes older Christians who have been in a church for five or more years. The veterans seem to be the most prone and susceptible. One telltale symptom heralding the presence of this disease is that we begin to think our own spiritual maturity is measured by how many faults we can detect in others. If I spot more faults than anyone else, then obviously I'm more spiritually mature.

But watch out! Because if you are looking for cursing, curses will find you!

> He also loved cursing, so it came to him; and he did not delight in blessing, so it was far from him (Ps. 109:17).

If you are not looking for what's good, then even what good there is present will be difficult to recognize.

CHANGE YOUR DEFINITION

One way to cultivate staying power is to change your definition of an event or circumstance. After all, the way in which you define your circumstances will determine, to a large degree, how you will respond to that event.

CONSIDER IT ALL JOY, AND WATCH YOUR FAITH GROW.

I lived in Eugene, Oregon, for many years. Eugene is known for, among other things, frequent gray skies and rain. Being from Hawaii, the absence of the sun's warm rays on my body took a toll on me, especially during the winter. Believe it or not, I actually resorted to buying a sunlamp one year when I felt I was about to die from a lack of solar exposure!

I remember walking to a coffee shop with a friend one November morning when it began to rain. Not looking forward to another rainy day, I complained, "Rain again! I wish it would quit."

My friend's response surprised me. "Hooray!" he cheered exuberantly. "Rain. I love it."

"Why in the world are you celebrating this horrible weather?"

"Because that means it's snowing in the mountains. Ski season has begun!"

My friend was an avid skier. He had defined "rain" as heralding the beginning of a great ski season. I, on the other hand, had defined it as cause for another day of depression and sunlamp therapy. Between each event and your attitude concerning that event lies your *definition* of that event.

> Consider [define] it all joy, my brethren, when you encounter various trials (Jas. 1:2).

James instructs us to define our events carefully because how we see our circumstances will affect our attitudes and actions. Not only does James tell us to define them carefully, but he also tells us to define it all as *joy!* Not just the good times but *all* of our circumstances, including trials, are to be defined as cause for joy.

How can we possibly do that? Read on, as James continues:

> Consider [define] it all joy, my brethren, when you encounter various trials, knowing that the testing of your faith produces endurance. And let endurance have its perfect result, that you may be perfect and complete, lacking in nothing (Jas. 1:2-4).

We get to define it *all* as joy, even our trials, when we know the positive outcome any event can have on our lives—deepening our faith, producing endurance and making us complete and lacking nothing. Wow! Now that's a powerful promise!

Change your definition, considering it all joy, and watch your faith grow, your endurance increase and your life become complete. You'll lack for nothing, simply because you've chosen to define things the way God defines them.

DEFINE THINGS THE WAY GOD DEFINES THEM

David is one of my heroes. He was one of Israel's greatest leaders, a man after God's own heart (see 1 Sam. 13:14). David faced many challenges, but he seemed to rise above every one! Even when his foes were far bigger, something always seemed to carry him through. How was he able to do this? David was a man who defined things, not as he saw them, but as God saw them.

When David was still a young shepherd and Israel was at war with the Philistines, he faced his most famous challenge. Instead of the two armies waging full-scale battle, each side agreed to choose its finest, most spartan warrior and let the two of them duke it out, each on behalf of his entire army. The winner would bring victory to his entire nation, while the nation of the loser would become slaves to the nation of the winner.

A giant named Goliath was chosen to represent the Philistines. He towered over the men of Israel, measuring over nine feet tall. His armor weighed more than 100 pounds. I'll bet he was uglier than sin, too.

Goliath made such an impression that every Israelite warrior cowered in fear (see 1 Sam. 17:24). They darted behind rocks, hid in caves and ducked behind bushes. Goliath stood on a hill like a bully, taunting the Israelites and cursing them by his gods.

David saw the giant making fun of the trembling Israelites, who were hiding in the thickets. Despite having a clear view of the situation, David defined the Israelites as "the armies of the living God" (1 Sam. 17:26).

They sure didn't look like warriors of an almighty God! They looked more like a bunch of chickens that had just seen a fox, or perhaps a flock of turkeys the night before Thanksgiving. If David had described the situation according to how it looked, he might well have defined these men as wimps. Instead, he called them the armies of the living God.

David walked up to his overgrown, unruly opponent and exclaimed, "You come to me with a sword, a spear, and a javelin, but I come to you in the name of the LORD of hosts, the God of the armies of Israel, whom you have taunted" (1 Sam. 17:45).

Righteous indignation filled his soul, and courage flooded his veins. David withdrew one of the five smooth stones in his bag, loaded his slingshot and let it fly! His years of practice on the back side of the desert paid off, and the stone caught the giant right between the eyes.

The giant muttered, "Boy, nothing like this ever entered my mind before," and he fell on his face to the ground. (The muttering part is paraphrased. You won't find it in your Bible, but it's in mine. I wrote it in the margin. I believe it's the first recorded case of a splitting headache recorded in the Bible.)

David chose to see things the way God saw them. And because he made this critical choice, God was able to use David to overcome impossible circumstances and lead His people to an overwhelming victory against the Philistines. So great was the victory that we still speak of it even today!

A second example of David defining things as God does is found in 1 Samuel 24. Some time after the Goliath incident, David found himself running from the wicked King Saul who wanted to take the young warrior's life. Saul's short-lived gratefulness to David for slaying the giant had turned into long-term jealousy. Although David was innocent, Saul's insecurity had driven him to rid his throne of any possible competitors, and yet David kept looking for the best in Saul, in spite of it all.

CULTIVATE A SPIRIT OF GRATEFULNESS, REGARDLESS OF YOUR CIRCUMSTANCES.

It was in the cave of Engedi where David displayed a quality of leadership that was to become a hallmark of his life. He was hiding in the cave when Saul entered, unaware of David's presence. Weary from his pursuit of David, Saul fell asleep. Here was David's golden opportunity to rid himself of Saul and end the king's merciless crusade! David's men urged him on:

> And the men of David said to him, "Behold, this is the day of which the LORD said to you, 'Behold; I am about to give your enemy into your hand, and you shall do to him as it seems good to you.'"
>
> So [David] said to his men, "Far be it from me because of the LORD that I should do this thing to my lord, *the LORD'S anointed*, to stretch out my hand against him, since *he is the LORD'S anointed*" (1 Sam. 24:4, 6, emphasis mine).

Let me ask you, did Saul deserve to be called the Lord's anointed? Did he act like the Lord's anointed? Obviously not!

But then again, did the Israelites, dismayed by a bully's threats and fleeing in every direction, resemble the army of the living

God? Surely this was a misnomer! Yet despite David's seeming blindness to the obvious, God gave David victory over his enemies and made him Israel's greatest leader.

Here's the gem: *David chose to define things as God defined them.*

David chose to see circumstances and events from God's perspective, and in so doing, he received strength and courage from the Lord. His "eye was clear" (see Matt. 6:22). His perspective was God-pleasing. This is why God made David successful in all he did. That kind of strength comes only as a result of having the right attitude!

David was a man after God's own heart, because he defined events the way God defined them.

DON'T MESS UP INSIDE THE FATHER'S HOUSE

Many of us suffer from the malady of an attitude trained by our circumstances rather than by the Spirit of God. When that happens, we begin to resemble the elder brother in the story of the prodigal son found in Luke 15. His younger brother had taken his inheritance and squandered it, and now after seeing the error of his ways, was returning home. Their father, overjoyed at the return and repentance of his prodigal son, called his elder son to rejoice with him.

But he became angry, and was not willing to go in; and his father came out and began entreating him. But he answered and said to his father, "Look! For so many years I have been serving you, and I have never neglected a command of yours; and yet you have never given me [one young goat], that I might be merry with my friends; but when this son of yours came, who has devoured your

wealth with harlots, you killed the fattened calf for him"
(Luke 15:28-30).

Sounds like sour grapes, doesn't it?

The prodigal had indeed messed up his life outside the father's
house. However, because of a bad attitude, his elder brother messed
up his life *inside* the father's house. Instead of looking for what he
could be grateful for, he found a reason that could justify his anger.

You see, if you look hard enough and wait long enough, you
can always find reasons that will justify your complaints. If you
compare yourself with others often enough, and investigate
what's fair or unfair, somewhere along the line you will surely find
that your "rights" have been violated, or you will find some other
reason to be offended.

Looking for what is bad in life can cause a person to develop
a deadly cancer known as ungratefulness. Ungratefulness affects
our attitude in subtle ways that may not surface for years, as in
the case of the prodigal son's brother. Because of his perspective,
which was focused entirely on himself and his problems, he
couldn't see the situation the way his father saw it. Because of his
bad attitude, the young man refused to welcome back his brother,
and he missed the blessing.

We do the same thing sometimes. Instead of seeing things as
our Father sees them and welcoming home a wayward brother or
sister, we begin to judge or complain, saying, "Hey, what about
me? What about all the time that *I* was faithful?" Our Father
wants us to join Him in welcoming back those who have
suffered outside His house. More importantly, He wants to make
sure that our hearts are right, so we don't miss His blessing.

Our behavior can cause us to mess up our lives *outside* the
Father's house, but our attitude will cause us to mess up our lives
inside the Father's house.

Both are devastating.

CULTIVATE A GRATEFUL SPIRIT

In *everything* give thanks; for this is God's will for you in Christ Jesus (1 Thess. 5:18, emphasis mine).

Cultivate a spirit of gratefulness, regardless of your circumstances. Not just when things are going your way, but in everything! Grateful attitudes never develop automatically. We must cultivate them and train them according to God's directions, much like programming a computer. If we set ourselves up with the right programming, we will get the right results. Wrong programming, wrong results. No programming, no results. The good news is we can program our attitudes with gratitude so that we can reap wonderful results.

You see, gratefulness is a spirit, an attitude, not a response to gifts and favors given to you. Learn the secret of being thankful for what God has already done for you, regardless of how things may appear to you right now. Cultivate this spirit *before* you receive any favors, *before* you win the sweepstakes, *before* someone is kind to you.

We find the following in the book of Psalms:

The lines have fallen to me in pleasant places (Ps. 16:6).

We will be satisfied with the goodness of Thy house, Thy holy temple (Ps. 65:4).

David wrote these lines of gratitude even as he was a fugitive, hiding from a powerful king intent on killing him. Though persecuted by Saul, young David was grateful for the protection and the sustaining hand of God.

The "lines" that had fallen to him in pleasant places signified the fact that David knew he had limitations on his life. Some things were simply out of his control and jurisdiction, and yet he was grateful. He considered the parameters, or limitations, God placed on him to be pleasant. You see, David's perspective on life, his attitude of excellence, is what gave him the edge.

You and I can cultivate the same kind of attitude.

Life is like a garden. You will only grow what you cultivate. Gratefulness will come when you cultivate it in the soil of your life.

TAKE THE TIME TO APPRECIATE

The Grand Canyon is one of the most awe-inspiring sights in the world, stretching for miles and miles. It is as though God scooped out a vast divide with His hand and sprinkled hues of beautiful rainbow colors, indelibly etching them into the granite and rocks. You can stand on the rim of the canyon and watch eagles soaring beneath you. The Grand Canyon truly is one of God's greatest masterpieces this side of heaven.

Some years ago, I took some kids from a youth group in Oregon on a trip to experience the Grand Canyon. Our journey involved 80 screaming kids jam-packed into seven vans. I had been driving for two days to share with them one of Earth's greatest natural wonders. After an arduous trip, we finally arrived, tired but filled with anticipation.

We jumped out of the van and hurried to the lookout point. Stepping up to the observation railing, we were met by a hot thermal rushing over our faces. The wind blew our hair straight back, and we could see the eagles soaring. *Wow!* I thought. *This is beautiful! I could stay here all day!*

After three or four minutes, the kids looked at me and said, "All right! That was nice. Let's go!"

I said, "Let's go? Look at this view. It's incredible!"

"Yeah, it's nice, Wayne, really nice. Now, let's go find a McDonald's."

I screamed, "Wait! You kids will stay here. You will enjoy this. You will remain here and enjoy this for at least 10 minutes. I did not travel for two solid days to leave after 3 minutes and go to McDonald's! You will like this. You will open your eyes and just look!"

What I may have failed to realize was that these kids were raised on television and that they had seen the Grand Canyon many times before. Through the technological marvel of a small video camera mounted on a hang glider's aluminum frame, these kids had, by proxy, flown over and through the great crevasse, capturing its beauty from a thousand different angles. They had seen the canyon through the lens of history as a geologist allowed them the vantage point of his mind's eye. They had seen it from the perspective of rafters on a white-water excursion, cutting through the canyon's river beneath the varicolored cathedral rising above.

Although this was their first actual experience, standing at a lookout point, compared to what they had seen on TV and movie screens, I guess it wasn't all that great! Our perch provided us with only one narrow viewpoint.

The Talmud, a book of Jewish writings, says, "God is going to hold us accountable for all the things that He put on this earth for us to enjoy and we didn't take time to do so." In training your eyes to see what is good, take the time to enjoy the simple things again. Pause long enough to smell the flowers. Stop long enough to sit down and see a sunrise or a sunset. Cultivate gratefulness.

When you do, you'll begin to condition your attitude, to cultivate a grateful spirit, and you will soon have a garden blooming with contentment.

LEARN TO ENJOY THE RIDE

One of the ways the Lord has trained my heart to cultivate gratefulness is by teaching me to enjoy this ride called life. There are going to be challenges and hills to climb on this journey. That's a given. Once you know that hills and trials will always be there, you will be able to expect them and no longer be surprised by them, which will free you up and enable you to enjoy the ride.

GOD HAS GIVEN US A BEAUTIFUL WORLD TO LIVE IN, A WORLD FILLED WITH HIS WONDERS, HIS PEOPLE AND HIMSELF.

God created things for us to enjoy. Stop and enjoy them. Enjoy life. Enjoy the sunshine. Enjoy the rain. When you go home, enjoy your meal. When your wife says, "Please mow the lawn, Dear," enjoy mowing the lawn! Take the dog for a walk. Enjoy the walk and enjoy your time with your dog. This life is too short for us to not enjoy it. Enjoy the ride.

The Bible says the joy of the Lord is our strength (see Neh. 8:10). But we often limp weakly through life because we have forgotten to take along our joy. God has packed it for us, but we forget to take it along. For every journey, every activity in your day, take along a fresh pack of joy.

One summer, our family went to Disneyland. One of the attractions my son wanted to check out was the Indiana Jones ride. I said, "Let's go for it!" Now, I'm an analytical person, and I watch stuff. As we were working our way through the line I said,

"See that, Aaron? See that little creature on the rock? It's not really a creature at all. It's a mechanical device that's computer activated."

"Really?" he asked.

"Yeah! And see the shapes on the wall? They're made by a light projected through a special filter. That filter's called a gobo. See it?"

"Oh, yeah!" said Aaron. "Cool. Cool."

Spurred further by his interest, I continued. "See that rock face over there, with the mist gliding across it? That's smoke coming from a machine, not really morning mist at all."

"Really?"

"Yeah. And see that over there, Son?"

"Uh-huh."

"That's a mirror."

"Really?"

We climbed into the car. "Do you see how this jeep is painted to look old, Aaron?"

"Yeah."

"It's brand-new, though. Check out the serial number."

"Yeah, it is!"

"And look under the dash. There aren't any wires. You know why? Because it's on a track." As I was transforming into a combination of Mr. Spock and Sherlock Holmes, the jeep lunged forward and we were in motion. The speed increased, and we whipped around a corner, eliciting screams from the girls in the car next to us.

"That was good, Aaron, but if it was banked another 10 degrees, the G-force would have been better. It really would have made your stomach drop!"

"Great, Dad!" said Aaron, having to shout in order to be heard.

"You see that, Aaron? That's another mirror!" I yelled, as we zipped down the track.

By this time, Aaron wasn't responding to my cogent analysis of the ride. He was midflight, with his head and body being jostled, twisted and pulled with every turn of the track.

"See that rock coming at us? It's on a track!" I yelled. "It'll go back and get reset for the next car behind us! Not very effective, huh?"

Soon the jeep came to a halt and the ride was over. "You know, Aaron, if we could have made a sharper turn on that second hairpin, it would've been even better. And if the smoke had come out sooner, we could have traveled right through it."

Aaron stopped me with a less than gracious tone, "Hey, Dad! Enough!"

"What do you mean, 'enough'?"

Without answering, he turned and stalked off. "Hey, you, get over here. I've got more things to tell you," I called after him. He kept walking.

"Enough!" he called back. "I ain't riding with you no more!"

"Okay. I'll meet you later!" I said. Then, under my breath, I muttered to myself, "Dumb kid! He just doesn't listen, does he? That's his problem."

As I was walking around kicking the dirt, the Lord spoke to my heart: "You missed the whole ride, didn't you? You were so busy trying to figure everything out, you missed the whole ride."

I stopped and thought, *You know, that's right! I don't even remember the ride. I was so involved in all the little details, I missed the whole ride!*

Have you ever done that? Have you ever gotten so caught up in the details of life that before you know it, the ride is over? Ever get so caught up in the preparations of a wedding that you miss the wedding? Ever get so distracted with cleaning the house before guests arrive that you alienate your whole family in the process? So often we are short with others, blaming our families and hissing at our neighbors in times of stress. We're like Martha, who was so "distracted with all her preparations" that she began to complain. Turning to her honored houseguest, Jesus, she exploded, "Lord, do You not care that my sister has left me to do all the serving alone? Then tell her to help me" (Luke 10:40). We get so distracted with the little details, we forget to enjoy the ride!

We miss the sunrises and sunsets, too often our children grow up without us, and the beauty of this ride called life goes unnoticed. My own children have grown up so quickly! Seems they were in diapers just a few days ago. Then all too quickly they were walking across the platform to receive their high school diplomas! The next minute they're gone, and the ride is over.

We begin our days with a jolt of coffee, motor from task to task, and return home exhausted—only to get up and do it all over again. Don't miss the ride! Instead of driving through at a relentless pace, let's slow down. God has given us a beautiful world to live in, a world filled with His wonders, His people and Himself. It's all there, if we will only take the time to enjoy.

It's taken me a while to learn this essential lesson. And I'm so glad I finally caught it! Here are a few ways I've learned to enjoy the ride:

1 Take five minutes today and write down the names of two people you appreciate. They may be people who have gone unnoticed. They could be a spouse, a friend or someone who did a good deed that slipped by everyone's notice. Write them a note of thanks. Be sure to add as much detail as you can about how that person's actions blessed you. And send it!

2 Don't forget to laugh. Some of us need to learn to laugh again. There is plenty to laugh about in life, and we need to laugh. Stand naked in front of a mirror. That alone should take care of your laughter

quota for a day or two. Keep a record of how many times you laugh today. It could be for any reason at all, but try to laugh at least five times! You'll find great opportunities by listening to children or spending a few more minutes in the lunchroom with your coworkers. If that's not working, go into the bathroom (again!) and imagine you're entering a funny-face contest. Practice before a mirror. (Be sure no one else is in the restroom at the time! You might want to check all the stalls before proceeding.)

3   Do one thing for yourself today. Write it into your schedule. Often I will stop on the way home at a little yogurt shop for a frozen treat. Oh, the ecstasy of those few minutes! This slows me down before I arrive home. For you, it could be a short jog, a walk or listening to some of your favorite music. Whatever it is, take time to enjoy life in its simplest form.

4   Make a new friend today. If you were given an assignment to make a new friend, how would you do it? It only takes a few minutes to stop and truly be interested in another person's life. Ask that person about his or her family, dreams or struggles. Then listen. Truly listen. You'll be surprised how many friends you will collect over a period of just a few days! By the way, a great place to start is with your family. You'll be surprised how many of us are related but not friends. Life is too short for that. By establishing deep friendships with your family, you'll begin to reap one of God's greatest promises and rewards.

Pause long enough to enjoy the ride. Train yourself to see what is good. Take the time to laugh with each other. Laugh at yourself. Although there will be imperfections and periodic setbacks, you will be surprised how wonderful life can be when you have a good attitude.

You will hear God better. You will enjoy His presence.

You will be pleasantly surprised how a new perspective will help you to develop an attitude that attracts friends, laughter, joy and success!

CHAPTER FOUR

RAISE THE BAR OF EXCELLENCE

If the axe is dull, and one does not sharpen the edge,

then he must use more strength.

ECCLESIASTES 10:10, *NKJV*

Developing your attitude is like developing your skill on a musical instrument—it takes consistent practice to improve.

When the great Polish pianist Ignacy Jan Paderewski was elected prime minister of his country, he made one request before accepting the prestigious office. He would lead the country, but he must be allowed to practice his scales for two hours every day. Guitar virtuoso Andrés Segovia requires the same of his students—two hours a day of playing scales.

And yet, who plays scales in a concert? You've never heard a composition by Mozart or Brahms called "The Aeolian Scale" or "Major Scale." However, without being thoroughly familiar with scales, a musician would remain remedial in his or her art. It is the complete mastery of the basics that gives birth to freedom of expression, ease of movement and cohesiveness in the delivery of each phrase.

DO SOMETHING TO "EXCEL STILL MORE" FOR THE SAKE OF THE KINGDOM.

So it is with each of us in our attitudes. Though we may have excelled in our approach to life, we must continue to develop every day. We need to practice having an excellent attitude in each and every endeavor, for it will always be true that we can improve the way we see problems, people and life.

After World War II, General Douglas MacArthur went to Japan to evaluate the rebuilding of the war-torn nation. The economy of Japan was in dire straits; the nation was struggling, having to use leftover resources just to stay afloat. As a result, any toy or appliance labeled "Made in Japan" was to be a trademark for one thing: poor quality. So General MacArthur brought in one of America's leading quality-control experts, Dr. W. Edward Demming.

After much evaluation and scrutiny, Demming came up with a set of business principles to help turn around Japan's economy. He called the country's most influential businessmen together and offered them a promise. He basically said, "If you will improve something about yourself and your product every day and make quality not merely something to be maintained but an achievement and a way of living, you will turn the economy of Japan around in 10 years. Then if you continue to improve something each day, even if it is a miniscule amount, in three decades you will become an economic world power."

That was quite a tall promise to make to this struggling nation, but they took it, hook, line and sinker. They even coined a new word for this approach: *kaizen*. The word means a constant, ever-increasing improvement that defines quality not as something to be maintained but something to be lived on a daily basis.

Over the next 10 years, the businesses of Japan did exactly that. They examined the American automobile; then they improved on it and sold it to American consumers. People began buying everything Japan produced because of the improved quality. Japanese ingenuity increased, and they improved on existing brands of appliances, electronics, tools, cameras and watches. Soon their products were in demand the world over.

In 10 years, the economy of Japan had reversed itself, and within three decades the country had become an economic world power. To this day, one of the most prestigious business awards is the W. Edward Demming Award.

If a change in attitude can do that for a nation's economy, how much more should we seek to do the same as builders of the kingdom of God?

Change Your Attitude for the Sake of the Kingdom

We request and exhort you in the name of the Lord Jesus that, as you received from us instruction as to how you ought to walk and please God (just as you actually do walk), *that you may excel still more* (1 Thess. 4:1, emphasis mine).

What is Paul saying in this passage? Keep on improving for the sake of the Kingdom. Be willing to improve. Be willing to get better.

Even if it's only 1 percent each day, improve something about yourself. Sharpen something! If you can improve just 1 percent a day, that means over one year you will have improved more than 300 percent for the kingdom of God. Just 1 percent a day!

> LET US ALSO LAY ASIDE EVERY
> ENCUMBRANCE, AND THE SIN WHICH
> SO EASILY ENTANGLES US, AND LET
> US RUN WITH ENDURANCE THE RACE
> THAT IS SET BEFORE US.
>
> HEBREWS 12:1

Look for something to improve about yourself. It may be the way you stand or comb your hair or something to improve your hygiene. It could be the way you shake hands or the way you look people in the eye when you talk with them. It may be something about your posture or your speech. Instead of responding to requests by muttering, "Yeah, okay," say, "Sure, I would love to!" When someone asks for your help, instead of replying, "I guess so," say, "I would be more than honored to help!"

Where can you improve? Perhaps it's in your discipline, the way you treat your spouse or the way you speak of your faith. Do something to "excel still more" for the sake of the Kingdom. Improve yourself 1 percent a day, for one year and see how much you grow! Raise the bar!

REALIZE THE POTENTIAL INSIDE YOU

I played club soccer at the University of Oregon, where the scrimmage field happened to be in the middle of a practice track. All around us, athletes would be practicing the high jump, pole vault, triple jump and other track and field events. (Incidentally, Eugene is a mecca for track and field. In fact, that's where Nike got its start).

I remember being intrigued by a persistent high jumper. One day he was practicing for a prestigious track meet that was eight months away. The bar on the high jump was set at 5'9". Now, 5'9" is taller than I am, so for me that is high! He made his attempt and cleared the bar. I looked at him and thought, *Wow! That's amazing! No springs, no pogo stick. He just jumped!* If I ever cleared the bar at 5'9", I would retire. I would take a picture of myself next to the bar at that height, buy myself the biggest trophy I could afford and brag endlessly to my kids. Not this athlete. Instead of retiring, he raised the bar and jumped again. He jumped 5'10" and instead of being satisfied, he raised the bar again. He did this for eight months!

Finally, the day of the track meet arrived. I bought a ticket for the event just to watch the high jumper who had become the object of my interest during the past eight months. The stadium was packed when the high-jump competition began. Many of the high jumpers faulted early, failing to clear the bar at 6'1" and 6'2". Finally, the bar was set at 6'4". My high jumper was the final contestant. He would be given three chances to clear 6'4", and if he did, he would win the competition.

He set out on his first attempt, but he hit the bar, falling to the ground with the bar in tow. On his second attempt, he again dislodged the bar. The crowd grew nervous with anticipation as he faced his third and final attempt. I can still recall him consulting with his coach, probably about the thrust of his head, the arch of his back or the timing of his foot. When he had mentally gone through each step and every maneuver, he returned to the field. He stared at the bar as if he were striking a deal with it.

After what seemed like an eternity, the young man nodded slightly and started his long, semicircular run toward the bar. Then, with every ounce of his conditioned strength and power, he planted one foot into the ground and launched into his final jump. Every tendon and joint stretched tight as he catapulted his body into the air. He thrust his head toward the clouds; his back arched in a precise curve over the top of the bar, his foot flicked at the precise moment, and he began his descent. *He had cleared the bar!*

His teammates rushed out of the grandstands, cheering. Caught up in the emotion of the moment, I found myself crying and running toward the champion saying, "You don't even know me, but I want to give you a hug!" His feat was amazing to me! I remembered his attempting to clear 5'9". But all the while, there was inside of him the potential of clearing 6'4"! *Yet he would never have realized that potential unless he had been willing to raise the bar.*

Some of us today are jumping at 2'6" in our daily lives. We figure that's good enough. But God says, "Inside of you, there is the potential of 6'4". What are you doing at 2'6"?"

Some of you might respond, "Not me! I'm a 2'6" kind of person." But God knows there is so much more inside you! Much more! But in order to achieve more, you must be willing to raise the bar.

God does not insist that we raise the bar a foot at a time. One inch is fine. This means incrementally increasing your abilities. Keep improving yourself for the sake of the kingdom of God, whether it be the depth of your faith, the way you treat people or the way you think. Improve these by 1 percent every day, and the potential God has placed in you will begin to emerge.

But first you must be willing to raise the bar.

BREAK THROUGH QUITTING POINTS

Among the things that war against our excelling still more are our individual quitting points—points where we tend to give up. This is where some person or task tests your patience to a certain limit and you say, "That's it! I'm through." This can happen on our jobs, in dealing with our children or in our struggles with temptation. Every single one of us has quitting points. What are some of yours?

Maybe you have a low tolerance for problems in relationships. When things are running smooth, everything's fine. But what happens when the temperature begins to rise and the two of you don't see eye to eye on things like you used to? You feel the heat. Finally, when the relationship thermometer hits 104 degrees (or 98 or 84), you say, "That's it! I'm not taking this anymore. I'm out of here!"

When we reach a certain level of physical, emotional or mental pain, we reach a quitting point and our systems begin to shut down. This quitting point can be the result of past habits, or it may simply be our predetermined tolerance level for problem solving. Whatever the cause, we bail out with predictable consistency at that certain quitting point.

On a pain threshold of 1 to 10—1 being "no pain at all" and 10 being "extremely painful"—how do you do? When a situation gets to be a 4, is that your quitting point? When someone gives you trouble or doesn't accept your suggestions, when things don't go exactly the way you want them to, do you start counting, "One, two, three, four! That's it! I'm through!" and bail out?

The devil is shrewd. He may be defeated, but he's not stupid. He is crafty and deceptive, and he would love nothing better than to take down as many of God's children as he can before his time is up. And you can bet that he knows your quitting points.

I'll bet Satan has statistical records on each of us, like a college football coach keeps on the players of opposing teams. He has a file with your name on it, and in this file is a graph plotting all your common quitting points. He keeps a running tally of these things. The devil knows if, on a pain threshold of 1 to 10, you bail out at 5.5 every time. So how does he use that information against you?

WATCH OUT—SATAN'S GOT YOUR NUMBER

The devil knows that whatever you need to do to sidestep pain or consequences, you'll do it. Even if it means going against your faith, your family or God's plans for your future. If you are unwilling to break through your quitting points, you will let the avoidance of pain become your god. Then all the devil needs to do is cause some rumblings, a little seismic activity in your life, to begin to undermine your resolve. It could begin with a minor complaint or a criticism about your weight or performance that demoralizes a relationship. It could be further damaged by the loss of someone close to you that you refuse to release. Your frustration may be further exacerbated by a financial loss or health setback. Soon the thermometer reaches 104 degrees, and you know what's coming next. Some people simply bail out, others blow up in anger, while others use their circumstances as an excuse to dive into the bottle or an affair.

One measure of a man or a woman is what it takes to get him or her to bail out of a commitment, whether it be a marriage, a friendship or a faith. What is the threshold of your quitting point?

> For you have need of *endurance* so that when you have done the will of God, you may receive what was promised (Heb. 10:36, emphasis mine).

Circle the word "endurance" in your heart and mind, for you need endurance to break through those quitting points and keep moving forward.

Make a decision now to change. Increase your capacity to deal with problems and discover how much more fruitful life can be.

PAY THE PRICE TO BUILD CHARACTER

The deeper your character, the easier it will be for you to develop an attitude of excellence. In fact, if you wish to experience success and fruitfulness in life, character is a necessary foundation. Without it, you will never survive success.

Although God desires success for each of us, success comes with inherent pitfalls to which the flesh is vulnerable. If there is in you a shallowness of character, you will easily fall prey to the clutches of pride, avarice, greed or the abuse of power.

So how do you develop character?

We want the good things of life handed to us on a silver platter. But there is a price to pay for godly character. God uses trials and lean times to mature you spiritually and to develop in you the character necessary for you to be fruitful in your relationships and finances.

By this is My Father glorified, that you bear much fruit, and so prove to be My disciples (John 15:8).

Imagine you owned a four-karat diamond worth thousands of dollars. This beautiful diamond is delicately displayed in a setting made up of five or six fingers called prongs. If the prongs are soft and prone to bending, then one sharp bump and the diamond is lost forever. A qualified jeweler would never mount such a stone in a weak setting.

The jeweler works diligently on the setting for each stone. When the diamond is polished and set, the fingers of the setting are made to tightly grasp the stone. The setting not only displays the radiant beauty of the diamond but also holds it fast. Then when the ring is bumped, the strong fingers won't let go.

Character is like the setting of a ring. If we do not allow God to build in us strong character, then we won't be ready for the success He wants to bring to our lives.

Character doesn't come cheap. It comes at a price—the price of digging your knees into the carpet, the price of studying, the price of suffering and the price of going through trials and discipline. We must be willing to pay the price. Let's look at what the apostle Paul says about the cost:

Everything else is worthless when compared with the priceless gain of knowing Christ Jesus my Lord. So, *whatever it takes,* I will be one who lives in the fresh newness of life (Phil. 3:8,11, *TLB*, emphasis mine).

Circle those three words in your heart, "whatever it takes." Be willing to pay the price for character, whatever it takes. And whatever it takes, let's be counted among those who live in the newness of life!

TO FEEL GOOD ABOUT YOURSELF: STAY CLEAN!

Keep yourself clean. I'm not talking about body odor; I'm talking about sin in your life. You can't feel good about yourself while living in sin. There just isn't any way. You also cannot feel good about yourself when you're tolerating sin. Repent as often as you need to in order to stay clean. Don't tolerate unresolved sin in your life. Remember, it's not just sin that destroys God's people—it's unresolved sin!

If I regard wickedness in my heart, the Lord will not hear (Ps. 66:18).

In the book of Joshua a man named Achan sinned by stealing things he knew were not his to take. Nevertheless, he sinned and then tried to hide it. He figured that if no one knew, nobody would be hurt.

The following day, the men of Israel went to battle and were duly routed by the enemy. Joshua was confused by the defeat because God had promised the Israelites victory over their enemies. Why had they been defeated? Joshua questioned God, who answered, "Israel has sinned . . . therefore the sons of Israel cannot stand before their enemies" (Josh. 7:11,12).

Further investigation revealed that Achan had disobeyed God's commands, and his unresolved sin had caused the army's weakness in battle. But once Achan's sin was revealed and the camp was cleansed, the Israelites again tasted victory.

You see, unresolved sin in your camp can cause you to miss out on God's blessings. Unresolved sin steals your confidence and causes you to have an attitude of defeatism and fear. So stay clean and remain in the flow of God's blessings.

One way we attempt to resolve sin is by renaming it. We change the word "sin" to something more tolerable:

- "It's an alternate lifestyle. What's wrong with being gay?"
- "We have a domestic partnership. Hey, sure we live together, but we love each other. We plan to get married someday."
- "It's just a social habit. I can quit anytime I want."

Let me share with you why this line of thinking is so dangerous. You see, there is no forgiveness for domestic partnerships. There's no forgiveness for an alternate lifestyle or addiction. There's only forgiveness for sin:

If we confess our sins, He is faithful and righteous to forgive us our sins and to cleanse us from all unrighteousness (1 John 1:9).

Until we say it's sin, forgiveness is not available to us. Can you see how important this is? Do you recognize the subtle strategy of the enemy to take the word "sin" and color it over and obscure it? We don't think we need forgiveness because we have justified the sin in our eyes.

Okay, but no one is perfect. We all slip here or there. But does that disqualify us? How do we keep ourselves clean?

KEEP A CLEAN HOUSE

My wife keeps a clean house, but that doesn't mean it never gets dirty. That would be impossible. Why? Because we have three kids! When I tell you my wife keeps a clean house, what I'm saying is this: Although our house gets messy, it doesn't stay that way very long before it gets cleaned up. And when it does get messy again, order is soon restored.

The same should be true of each of us. Though you stumble, fumble and fall, don't tolerate any unresolved situation. Don't live with it or let it stay that way for a long time. Clean it up.

You'll stumble. Clean it up.

You'll make a mistake. Clean it up.

You can't develop a godly attitude when you're living with unresolved sin. Stay clean!

Hudson Taylor was a missionary to China. He understood the importance of staying clean. He knew that a repentant person was a healthy person. A repentant church would be a healthy church. This was so important to him that when he greeted people during the day, he wouldn't shake their hands and ask, "How are you today?" Instead, he would shake their hands and ask, "Have you repented today?" Taylor was not trying to be condescending but rather to sincerely encourage people to stay clean!

God loves you and wants to forgive you. Forgiveness is abundantly available for sin. If you have sinned, say, "Lord, forgive me of my sin." God will not condemn you; He will invite you into His home, where He will shower you and cover you with His forgiveness. God never speaks to you in words of condemnation. He will always speak to you with words of invitation. That's the kind of God we serve.

Don't ever believe the lies of the devil, who paints God as a bad guy, a legalistic tyrant. God loves you! He died for you! Does that tell you how valuable you are to Him?

So stay clean. Stay within God's abundant grace and by doing so He will be able to continue building a diamond-quality character in you. With this character strongly in place, you will be ready for Him to set His greatest plan in your life. And in that, you will see evidence of a life that raises the bar of excellence!

CHAPTER FIVE

PLAY THE RIGHT BACKGROUND MUSIC

Speaking to one another in psalms and hymns and spiritual songs,

singing and making melody with your heart to the Lord.

EPHESIANS 5:19

God created every human being with a built-in surround-sound music system. It resembles the on-hold music you hear when you're waiting to talk to your doctor or the music that wafts through the mall to entice you to buy more.

WHATEVER IS TRUE, WHATEVER
IS HONORABLE, WHATEVER IS RIGHT,
WHATEVER IS PURE, WHATEVER IS
LOVELY, WHATEVER IS OF GOOD
REPUTE, IF THERE IS ANY EXCELLENCE
AND IF ANYTHING WORTHY OF
PRAISE, LET YOUR MIND DWELL ON
THESE THINGS.

PHILIPPIANS 4:8

Our internal music is composed of the thoughts we think over and over. These include selected memories—maybe something your mom or dad once said to you, a word of encouragement from a teacher or the way you felt when you weren't picked to be on the team or to be someone's friend. As you dwell on these memories, experiences and thoughts, they are recorded on the soundtrack of your mind and play continuously all day long.

Whatever you play on this internal sound system affects everything about you—your attitude, your self-image, your confidence level, your relationships, the way you communicate with others and even your faith.

Each of us gets to determine what music we are going to play. You are the disc jockey, choosing your own theme songs. Doesn't that seem wonderful? We get to play the music of our choice to accompany us throughout our day. We can choose from every grand sound track, opera or melodious composition ever written!

The reality is that most of us make some very odd musical choices. Some of our tapes and CDs have deep scratches on them. Some are so old, they're like the 78-rpm vinyl records of decades ago—old songs, old experiences that should long have been forgotten or forgiven.

Some people have been playing the same songs repeatedly for years. Do any of these theme songs sound familiar?

"It's my party and I'll cry if I want to . . ."

"Put your head on my shoulder . . ."

"What kind of fool am I . . . ?"

What have you chosen to be on the sound track of your life?

Think about it. What would a motion picture be without its sound track? Try watching the climactic ending of *Jaws* with the sound turned off. It's ridiculous! All you get is a rubber fish jumping onto a sinking boat.

But turn on the music, and the familiar rhythmic pounding of the arrangement makes your blood curdle, and your heart pumps in cadence with each beat. You begin to perspire when the string section crescendos. And when the horns blast, you take cover!

To this day I steer clear of any body of water for fear that a great white shark may be present! (I live on an island.) I even refuse to take baths in my tub as a direct, dysfunctional result of my moviegoing.

Memories hang on for a long time if you let them. They will play the selections attached to them, giving you feelings of fear or courage, insecurity or assurance.

You are the disc jockey. What is your play list? You get to make the selections, so choose wisely!

WHAT'S IN YOUR WALLET?

The way we steward our memories can be a major impediment to our developing a great attitude. Past experiences, as well as our perceptions of those experiences, are collected over the years. These are stored in what I call our internal photo album. Here your memories, like pictures, are catalogued for quick retrieval.

These photo albums are similar to the plastic picture holders we keep in our wallets or the albums we keep on the shelves in our family room—you know, the ones filled with pictures of our children, vacations, birthday parties, graduations and the like. The pictures that made it into these hallowed pages of fame represent only a fraction of the pictures actually taken. How did these specific pictures get the honor of holding the family's memories? What qualities earned each snapshot the privilege of being mounted in the family photo album?

Well, it works like this. The family member who is the first to arrive on the scene and thumb through the pictures recently returned from the developer becomes the judge of what pictures will actually make the cut. In our household, that person is usually me. (I plan it that way!)

Now the selection process begins. If, as I am thumbing through the 3x5-inch prints, I come across a picture that makes me look heavier than I really am, out it goes! It is usually discarded immediately without hope for a trial. Any photo snapped at the precise moment a forkful of food was entering my mouth is consigned to the dark abyss of my trash can. If there's one that shows me with my eyes closed, looking funny, with bad posture or anything else that might be conceived in the eyes of the beholder as less than optimal, it is whisked away without funeral or fuss.

Only those pictures that cause me to rival the best male models make it into the album! Then when someone pages through one of our commemorative displays, I look like I just stepped off a Hollywood set.

None of us would ever allow all the pictures into our albums. That would be horrible. And neither would we take the poorest of the pictures, place them neatly under each cellophane page and throw away all the best shots! That would be masochistic!

As silly as that sounds, that's often exactly what we do with our memories. We forget the best and remember the worst. We tuck the injuries away in the pages of our mental photo albums, and whenever we get the chance, we thumb through the pain again and again. If you could flip through most people's memory albums, you would probably find few prize pictures and many more painful ones.

DO YOUR MEMORIES GIVE YOU COURAGE OR STEAL IT?

It is absolutely critical that we steward our memories well. Why? The memories you choose to keep will either give you courage, or they will steal what courage you have. Your memories will either help to build your faith or plague you with doubts.

Has someone injured you in the past? You can either file a picture of the hurt in your album or discard it. If you choose to retain and rehearse the event, turning it over and over in your mind, it will affect you adversely. Each time you come into contact with this person, you will notice a distance growing between you. Your most strenuous attempts at conversation will prove shallow and insincere at best. Your memories have stolen your courage to resolve the problem and interact genuinely. On the other hand, when we store pictures of the wonderful moments shared with our loved ones, our courage is bolstered so that we can talk openly and honestly with them.

As he looked out upon the mighty Goliath, towering over the armies of Israel on the battlefield, young David drew courage from his memories of what God had done for him in the past. David confidently stood before his king and asked to be chosen for the task of defeating the giant, saying

> "Your servant has killed both the lion and the bear; and this uncircumcised Philistine will be like one of them, since he has taunted the armies of the living God ... The LORD who delivered me from the paw of the lion and from the paw of the bear, He will deliver me from the hand of this Philistine." And Saul said to David, "Go, and may the LORD be with you" (1 Sam. 17:36-37).

Where did this young lad find such courage and faith? From his mental photo album. David's confidence was based on his experiences and his memories of victory over the beasts of the field. And remembering this, David was able to see an impossible victory before it came to pass. His faith gave him confidence for things not yet seen and courage despite the things he could see.

Steward your memories well. What are you remembering each day? Are you a good steward of your memories? Or are you putting all the worst pictures into your album and discarding the best? Too many of us remember what we should forget, and we forget what we should remember.

Maybe it's time to do some spring cleaning. Go through the memories you've been keeping. Rummage through your old tapes and scratchy CDs. Take a few moments to write down the pictures you need to discard. Evaluate them one by one. Do you need to bury the hatchet? Do you need to extend forgiveness? Then do so and get rid of the bad memories!

Take a few minutes to bring your album into balance, so that you forget what you should forget and remember what you should remember. Build up your best memories, memories that give you courage. And as you replace the pages of your old albums with victorious new memories, you will begin to gain a new, God-given confidence that leads you to an excellent attitude!

WHAT DO YOU THINK?

How we steward what's happening inside our hearts and minds will affect the way we think. When we think clearly, we are more likely to have a healthy attitude toward the circumstances that come our way. If our thinking is muddled, our tendency will be to develop and display a poor attitude.

M. Scott Peck, in his book *People of the Lie*, tells about one of the Vietnam War's greatest tragedies, the My Lai massacre. One morning in March 1968, in the Quang Ngai province of South Vietnam, hundreds of innocent women and children were killed. The little village was known to have been harboring Vietcong soldiers. However, when an American task force arrived that day, they searched the village and found no enemy soldiers. But commanding officer Lieutenant William Calley was taking no chances. He ordered his troops to round up the villagers in groups of 20 to 30 and, with rifle fire or grenades, kill everyone until the village was eradicated.

Dr. Peck, a psychologist, was called in to investigate and try to determine what would make men perform an act of such senseless violence. He interviewed the soldiers as well as the officers involved. Peck concluded that the massacre wasn't necessarily motivated by vindictive or evil intentions. Rather, it was the tragic result of an unwillingness of the troops to think deeply about what was going on around them. They had their orders, and without consideration or forethought for the consequences, the American soldiers acted in a mindless, barbaric fashion.

Dr. Peck provides us with these poignant findings:

> As a people, we're too lazy to learn and too arrogant to think we needed to learn. We felt that whatever way we happened to perceive things was the right way without any further study. And whatever we did was the right thing to do without reflection.[1]

Too often our thoughts go no further than the initial perceptions that enter our minds. Rarely are we able to draw correct conclusions from this minimal input. To think that whatever just pops into our heads about a person or situation is always the truth would indeed make us a "people of the lie."

If your thinking is poor, so will your perspective be. And if your perspective is poor, so will your decisions be.

WHAT ABOUT THOSE FLEETING THOUGHTS?

John Wesley once quipped, "I can't stop a bird from flying over my head, but I sure can stop him from making a nest in my hair!" He was alluding to the fact that although wrong thoughts may pass through our minds from time to time, we shouldn't let them take up residence or give those wrong thoughts an audience. We may have little control over such fleeting thoughts, but we surely are responsible for the ones we allow to put down stakes and set up shop.

God requires each of us to judge and evaluate our thoughts and intentions. If they are not sound or biblical, then we must bring them into submission to God's Word. Just because a thought is lodged in your mind does not mean it belongs there! You must decide and steward the thoughts that are being housed in your heart and mind. If they don't fit into God's best, evict them!

We use our powerful God-tools for smashing warped philosophies, tearing down barriers erected against the truth of God, fitting every loose thought and emotion and impulse into the structure of life shaped by Christ (2 Cor. 10:5, *THE MESSAGE*).

In Ephesians 6:14-17, Paul describes the armor of God. He compares six pieces of a Roman soldier's armor to truths the Christian can apply in his or her life. Let's focus on one portion of the scriptural armor:

Therefore put on the full armor of God, so that when the day of evil comes, you may be able to stand your ground, and after you have done everything, to stand. Stand firm then . . . Take the *helmet of salvation* (Eph. 6:13,17, *NIV*, emphasis mine).

One of the soldier's main pieces of protection was his helmet, which the Bible calls the helmet of salvation. The Roman helmet was usually made of bronze or a bronze alloy, and it was virtually impenetrable. Fronted by a hinged visor to protect the soldier's face during battle, the helmet was de-signed to protect the neck as well, for in battle the soldier's neck would be a prime target for an opponent seeking to decapitate him.

So why do we need the helmet of salvation? If the adversary of our souls can find a Christian with an unprotected thought-life. he will easily find his mark. Satan is a headhunter, our minds are the battlefield, and our imaginations are his trophies.

Protect yourself well, guarding your thought-life and stewarding all that goes on in your mind. Then you will be able to stand your ground against Satan, against becoming a people of the lie. And when everything is done, you will be left standing, victorious.

WHAT DO YOU SEE THROUGH YOUR BELIEF WINDOW?

Hanging in front of every one of us is an invisible window through which we see the world around us. As we go through life, we view events, circumstances and people through this belief window.

As time goes on, different things are etched on our windows, and whatever is written will color or discolor what we view through that window. These things may be something wonderful, like God's promises; or they can be demeaning, like a remembered insult. What you see can resemble a beautiful mural or ugly graffiti, depending on what you choose to allow onto your window.

Your parents may have drummed into you that you're slow or irresponsible, and from that time forward, you've seen everything in light of that statement. "You'll never amount to anything," they may have said. Later in life when you made a mistake, you may have seen that situation in such a way that confirmed to you that you indeed are irresponsible and slow.

You can't always prevent people from spraying graffiti on your window, but you can decide whether or not to let it remain there!

You alone are responsible for what is written on that window—inside as well as out. You see, we have a tendency to scribble some pretty demeaning things on it ourselves! You must steward that window, clean it regularly and ensure that only those things that build you up remain there.

ARE YOU USING GOD'S WINDOW CLEANER?

The best way to ensure your thoughts are correct is to judge them by God's Word. If God wouldn't say it to you, then eradicate it without another thought. Don't hold a funeral for it, and don't dwell on it. If it doesn't build you up, then *whoosh!*—out it goes.

Discipline yourself to make a daily time for reading the Scriptures, even if only for a few minutes. God's Word will keep your belief window clean and your thoughts healthy. And, remember, healthy thoughts build healthy attitudes!

Nothing can equal the benefit of reading the Bible on a consistent basis. If the devil can keep you from the Word, he can keep you from realizing your full potential in life.

All Scripture is inspired by God and profitable for teaching, for reproof, for correction, for training in righteousness; that the man of God may be adequate, equipped for every good work (2 Tim. 3:16).

Let God's Word clean your perspective and mentor you in the ways of life. It will form your character and fashion your personality, shaping your attitude until it becomes the underlying foundation for fruitfulness in every area of your life.

Remember, poor thoughts equal poor attitudes. So be careful what you allow into your mind:

The lamp of the body is the eye; if therefore your eye is clear, your whole body will be full of light (Matt. 6:22).

What does it mean that the eye is the lamp of the body? I looked up the word "lamp" in my dictionary and here's the definition: "a device that generates light . . . for the purpose of illumination." A secondary definition said a lamp is "something that illumines the mind or soul." Wow! I like that definition even better.

EVERYTHING DEPENDS ON WHAT KIND OF TREASURE, GOOD OR EVIL, YOU DEPOSIT INTO YOUR HEART.

We receive much of our information about the world through our eyes. How we view the world affects our thoughts, and our thoughts affect our very souls. Jesus tells us we must keep our eyes, our windows, clear in order to enjoy a life filled with light.

Isn't it time you "trim the lamps" of your body, keeping your eyes from unclean things? Let God reveal the improper ways you think and cooperate with Him as you seek to develop attitudes that attract success.

Let us therefore, as many as are perfect, have this attitude; and if in anything you have a different attitude, God will reveal that also to you (Phil. 3:15).

WHAT IS IN YOUR HEART?

Watch over your heart with all diligence, for from it flow the springs of life (Prov. 4:23).

Proverbs gives us this gem of a truth we would do well to carefully consider. If we miss this or fail to understand its truth, we would do as well to build a sleek car with a powerful engine, pay to enter it in the Indianapolis 500 and hire a driver who doesn't know how to drive! Our heart is the seat from which all of life is affected, positively or negatively. And when we understand the immense power of our hearts, we as the drivers of that vehicle will be better able to operate it.

We find this truth in God's Word:

> For the mouth speaks out of that which fills the heart. The good man out of his good treasure brings forth what is good; and the evil man out of his evil treasure brings forth what is evil (Matt. 12:34-35).

What makes a heart healthy is what we feed it. The Bible calls this treasure-building. Whatever you put into your heart is exactly what will come out. It all depends on what kind of treasure, good or evil, you deposit into your heart. So set a sentry over your heart that allows only good treasure to be deposited!

> Finally, brethren, whatever is true, whatever is honorable, whatever is right, whatever is pure, whatever is lovely, whatever is of good repute, if there is any excellence and if anything worthy of praise, let your mind dwell on these things (Phil. 4:8).

The thoughts of our minds are important because they form the treasure that eventually makes its way into our hearts. If our treasure is good, we also will be good; but if our treasure is evil, we will be the same.

If you allow fearful thoughts to enter your heart, you will develop a fearful heart. You can have a hardened heart, a calloused heart, a shallow heart or a broken heart. It all depends on what you allow to enter.

You may have heard people say, "Boy, that really gets my goat!" or "That affected me so deeply" or "I just can't shake this feeling." These are phrases that indicate whatever was seen or heard was allowed into those people's hearts, the very seat of their affections. As a result, their perspectives were altered by it.

I like the way THE MESSAGE paraphrases Proverbs 4:23: "Keep vigilant watch over your heart; that's where life starts." Just because a thought crosses your mind does not mean it has permission to enter your heart. Judge your thoughts as to whether or not they are fit to enter your heart. If they are not, don't dare allow them entrance! Don't gather bad treasure. That's how broken hearts happen—they are not so much caused by our circumstances or by what others have said or done but rather by how many of these negative things we have allowed to build up in our hearts.

"Above all else, guard your heart, for it affects everything you do," says THE NEW LIVING TRANSLATION. Set a sentry over the lid of your heart, and don't open it indiscriminately. Do not allow entry to poisons, toxins, robbers and thieves. Judge every thought, and if it is unfit for your attention, flush it! We do that with other waste matter, so why not for wasteful thoughts?

WHO IS RUNNING YOUR CONTROL ROOM?

While I was in Bible college, I visited the local county jail from time to time. No, not to be admitted but to speak at chapel services. This jail was one of the most modern in the state. It was a keyless system—the doors were not manually operated but were opened and closed with an electronic system.

As I approached the door on my way to the chapel for the first time, a voice came over a loudspeaker: "May I see your identification, please?"

A bit startled by the faceless voice, I took out my driver's license and held it up. A camera recorded it and the voice continued, "What is your purpose here?"

"I am here to speak at the chapel," I answered, still bewildered.

The door opened, and I had started to enter when I remembered that I had no idea where to find the chapel.

"Excuse me," I said to the disembodied voice, "could you tell me how to get to the chapel?"

"Sure," the voice replied. "Just go through the opening doors, and I will lead you there."

I proceeded down the cement corridor, and before long a door opened to my left. Complying with my faceless instructor, I took a left turn and entered another hallway. Halfway down this corridor, an elevator door opened. Figuring my electronic tour guide was still leading me, I entered the elevator. To my surprise, I found that there were no buttons to push! Blank stainless steel walls greeted me as the elevator doors closed in front of me. The elevator began to ascend.

Star Trek! I thought to myself. *This is very strange.*

The elevator came to a stop, the doors silently opened, and there I was in the chapel. When the service was over, I asked one of the guards if I could see the control room where my faceless tour guide was housed. I followed the guard down several long corridors to a small room fully enclosed with bulletproof glass and equipped with several television monitors. A few men were monitoring every doorway and every room and, at their discretion, they allowed people in and out by pushing a few buttons.

I was intrigued by this new technology, but I also quickly saw its vulnerability. I thought to myself, *If the wrong person got into*

*this control room, he could wreak havoc on this whole place. He could control
everything!*

The heart is like a control room. For years, I pushed all the
levers and made all the decisions the way I thought they should
be made. I tried to handle my life on my own. When that didn't
work, I tried the world's way and things went from bad to worse.
When I realized my whole life was being adversely affected by my
attitude, like the prodigal son I finally came to my senses. I
opened the door of my heart to Jesus Christ and asked Him to
come into the control room of my heart. Only then did He begin
cleaning house and changing everything about me.

JESUS CAN HEAL YOUR BROKEN HEART. THAT'S WHAT HE CAME TO DO.

You see, God is a gentleman, and He never forces Himself on
anyone. Instead He knocks and extends the same invitation He
gave to me. He offers to dwell in your heart through faith (see
Eph. 3:17). It is the most eternal decision a person will ever
make, but He is available just for the asking.

When He enters, let Him have the controls. He isn't invited
in to watch *you* move the levers and press the buttons. You can't
ask Him into your heart so He can bring you good luck or
simply bless your efforts. *He enters to take over!*

Some may still say, "I know now to watch over my heart with
all diligence, but the damage has already been done. What can I
do if I have already let these thoughts enter? What if others'
words have already pierced my confidence and broken my heart?"

Please remember that Jesus came for people just like you! This was His assignment when the Father sent Him to bring redemption to fallen man:

The LORD has anointed me to bring good news to the afflicted; He has sent me to bind up the brokenhearted (Isa. 61:1).

Jesus can heal your broken heart. That's what He came to do. Ask Him. No one can heal hearts like Jesus can.

There's an old nursery rhyme that goes like this:

Humpty Dumpty sat on a wall,
Humpty Dumpty had a great fall.
All the king's horses and all the king's men
Couldn't put Humpty together again.

And I would add "But the King could. So the King Himself came down from heaven's throne and found all the Humpty Dumpties. Then with the care and compassion that only the King could have, He began to put them together again."

And He still does that today. You see, it was for all the broken lives, broken hearts and broken people that He died on Calvary.

You may think there are certain things you will never be able to forget. Or maybe you know things that seem beyond forgiveness. If you have come to just such an impossible impasse, let me encourage you with one cure-all. He's the only cure-all that really does cure all: Jesus. Only Jesus can heal all things, because He paid the price. He paid with His own blood to cover every sin, every hurt and even every thought. He offers us the power of His love, free for the taking, to cover our most valuable possessions— our eternity, our hearts and our minds.

Allow Jesus to mend your broken heart. Begin by replacing any broken thoughts with His Word. Then excavate any harmful memories, replacing them with His promises. And when you begin to accept the amazing grace He has offered, you will begin to see yourself in a whole new light. You will define your life the way He has defined it, according to His Word. As you allow Him to take you from glory to glory, you will begin to see your thoughts change, your heart become strong and your life be transformed.

When that begins to happen, you will add the most wondrous background music to your life. Listen very closely. It's the most beautiful symphonic sound track you'll ever experience!

Note

1. M. Scott Peck, *People of the Lie: The Hope for Healing Human Evil* (New York: Simon and Schuster, 1983).

CHAPTER SIX

PRACTICE, PRACTICE, PRACTICE!

But solid food is for the mature, who because of practice have their

senses trained to discern good and evil.

HEBREWS 5:14

As with learning any sport or musical instrument, the more you practice developing an attitude of excellence, the more proficient you'll become at it. Learning to develop a good attitude doesn't happen by accident. It needs to be intentional and deliberate— nothing less. Your first attempts may seem awkward, but keep practicing!

During my first year at college, I was walking down one of the hallowed halls and saw a huddled group of students congregating in a small circle. I was shy in those days, believe it or not. Being from Hawaii and of a different ethnicity, I was a bit self-conscious, so I was just going to keep walking.

Just then, the Lord spoke quietly to my heart: *Stop and introduce yourself to these students.*

All of what I am about to tell you happened within a few nanoseconds, but it left a lifelong impression on me. God doesn't need to use an English vocabulary when He speaks. In one atomic moment, He can deposit reams of instruction directly into your heart that will leave your life absolutely transformed.

But instead of changing, I was determined to argue with God. *No, that's not me, Lord. You know that's not me. I'm sort of to myself. I'll just pass by these students. They probably don't want me barging into their conversation anyway.*

I remember the Lord saying, *Do you want to remain what you are today and be that way the rest of your life, or do you want to become what I want you to be? The choice is yours. Right now, you're at a crossroads in your life.*

I sensed His urgency and knew that this was a moment that called for my best response. How often we miss these crossroad opportunities, and our future is the worse for it! I had to choose and to believe I could change.

Taking an immediate detour, I headed right into the middle of the crowd and introduced myself. "Hi! My name is Wayne

Cordeiro. I'm from Hawaii. I'm a freshman here at the college. How are you?"

To my surprise, they were gracious and welcoming. I still remember their acceptance and their love, and to this day a few of those students are some of my best friends.

PRACTICE UNTIL IT'S COMFORTABLE

Ask any backyard athlete that went on to be coached in a certain sport. Most of them had to change the way they held a baseball bat or shot a basketball or swung a golf club.

When I first played racquetball, it was against an old cement wall in high school. A group of us picked up some old, dilapidated racquets and started to play. We didn't care too much about form. We just wanted to have fun.

As time went on, I became a bit more serious about the game, so I entered a few tournaments. As much as I played, however, I could never advance beyond a certain level. One day, between matches, an instructor took me aside. He was one of the most renowned players and instructors on the racquetball circuit, so I welcomed his suggestions.

"Wayne, you have some natural talent at this game," he said, "but you'll never advance if you don't change your grip. Your form is incorrect."

Well, I had never heard *that* before. I asked him if he would give me a few lessons, and he agreed to meet with me the following week. Then I asked him what I might work on until we could get some lessons in.

He said, "The main problem impeding your progress is the way you're holding the racquet. Here, let me show you how to hold it properly."

He changed the way I had been gripping my racquet for the past 10 years! The new grip felt so awkward, I almost immediately dismissed it as useless. Sensing my uneasiness, he quickly added, "Even though this may seem uncomfortable, keep practicing until it becomes comfortable. And I guarantee, it will. So stay with it!"

Due to my respect for this instructor and his reputation, I changed my grip and went back to the tournament. I was soundly beaten in each of the games! Even with my best effort, I couldn't control the ball. I suspected this new grip was a sabotage effort by an opposing player who put the racquetball champ up to this heinous deed.

The following week, he and I got together for some lessons and I told him about my dismay over the new grip. "It's too awkward!" I complained. "What's wrong with my old grip?"

"You can use the old grip, but you'll never advance," he said. "If you want to play with the first graders and elderly, that grip will work just fine. But if you want to play with the big boys, you can't be holding your racquet that way."

That was enough to motivate me. I changed my grip!

But still it felt uncomfortable. He took me through some exercises I was to do each day. Over a period of a month, the new grip became as comfortable as the old one. Then I began to advance and improve again.

ACT IT BEFORE YOU FEEL IT

Have you ever seen a person with a wonderfully contagious attitude? When such people enter a room, the atmosphere changes. They can light up any gathering. Their presence is not a sham or a put-on—there's just something about them that's special.

Listen to these people talk on the phone. Watch the grace with which they deal with problem persons. Observe the way they stand, the way they sit, the way they lean forward slightly when they are listening to you, nodding in agreement.

Watch them. There's something different about their physiology. They sit straighter, they stand taller, and their smiles are genuine.

One of the easiest ways to practice developing an attitude that attracts success is to begin changing your physical posture. It's that simple! Soon you will find you have a tendency to feel the way you act.

Try slumping your shoulders and hanging your head for a few minutes. Talk like someone really depressed would talk. It won't be long before you'll feel awfully depressed!

Or put a smirk on your face, like someone with a really bad attitude would wear. Cock your hip and cross your arms. Look for problems like someone with a bad attitude would. I guarantee that before long, you'll be sporting a genuine, grade-A *bad* attitude!

Now think of someone you know who has a wonderful attitude. Sit how this person would sit. Speak up like a person with a wonderful disposition would speak. Respond with gentle yet affirming nods when someone is speaking to you. I assure you, it won't be long before you'll see signs of a wonderful attitude in yourself!

Even though it may feel a bit awkward to you at first, don't slump back into the old grip you've been using! Stay with the new, improved grip.

Keep practicing until it becomes comfortable!

PREPARE FOR THE METAMORPHOSIS

My children, with whom I am again in labor until Christ is formed in you (Gal. 4:19).

The word "formed" in this particular verse is the Greek word *metamorphon*. Here Paul is talking about the struggle that takes place until there is in us a metamorphosis—the old vanishes and the new emerges. It is the picture of a caterpillar becoming a butterfly. It is that process by which that beautiful creature on the inside finally makes its way to the outside!

Paul knew the potential of those Christians in Galatia to whom he was writing. Although he had taught them how to live, the knowledge inside their heads hadn't become evident in their behavior and lifestyles. They were still in the formation stage, and Paul had been living in painful anticipation until that which was known would become seen!

GOD'S BEST IS IN EACH OF US— HE CREATED US THAT WAY.

Think of a beginning tennis player. He has read all the magazines, watched the videos and studied the best players. He is focused on the smooth delivery of the serve. He can visualize the ball tossed gently into the air at a precise height, the tennis racket poised over his perfectly arched back and the smooth explosion that rifles the ball into the opponent's court.

Ace!

He has catalogued the perfect tennis form frame-for-frame in his mind. He can clearly visualize this artistic routine, but his actual demonstration of that routine is far from graceful! He throws the furry sphere higher than expected. The mistimed toss causes him to grunt in crude effort as he shoves the racket toward the dropping ball. He pushes it awkwardly toward the opposite end of the court, only to have it snagged by the net.

However, with adequate coaching and consistent practice, a graceful form begins to emerge. Little by little, we begin to see glimpses of a great tennis player inside! Then, as the days go by and the coaching continues, there begins a metamorphosis in which the inner becomes the outer. The young player's serve becomes increasingly more graceful. What he once only imagined he now is experiencing due to practice. What was once abnormal is now natural and comfortable.

When we see a player move like that, in tennis terms, we call that "great form." That's the same word spoken by Paul in the fourth chapter of Galatians to express what the Lord desires for each of us: ". . . until Christ is *formed* in you" (v. 19, emphasis mine). God's best is in each of us. He created us that way, but what's inside will take time to make its way into our outer form. That requires practice; but with a little determination and consistency, people will soon be calling you Ace.

CULTIVATE THE FRUIT OF THE SPIRIT

One of the best ways to practice is to cultivate the fruit of the Spirit—the character qualities the Holy Spirit builds within us—if we allow Him.

The fruit of the Spirit is love, joy, peace, patience, kindness, goodness, faithfulness, gentleness, self-control (Gal. 5:22-23).

Each character quality is something the Spirit of God wants to produce within us. This tells me that one of the best ways to cooperate with His working is to *practice* being loving, being joyful, keeping a heart of peace, and so forth. He is faithful to bear these fruits in our lives as we are faithful to practice them.

Take a moment to rate yourself on each of these characteristics. Which ones do you need to practice? (Hint: The areas you most need to practice are those that are least practiced now.)

Read each definition that follows. Then evaluate where you stand and determine which areas you need to prioritize for practice.

	Least Practiced					Most Practiced				
Love	1	2	3	4	5	6	7	8	9	10
Joy	1	2	3	4	5	6	7	8	9	10
Peace	1	2	3	4	5	6	7	8	9	10
Patience	1	2	3	4	5	6	7	8	9	10
Kindness	1	2	3	4	5	6	7	8	9	10
Goodness	1	2	3	4	5	6	7	8	9	10
Faithfulness	1	2	3	4	5	6	7	8	9	10
Gentleness	1	2	3	4	5	6	7	8	9	10
Self-control	1	2	3	4	5	6	7	8	9	10

Love

Am I consistently committed to helping others develop and discover God's very best in their lives? Do I treat others as God would treat them?

Joy

Do I trust the fact that God is in control of every situation, regardless of how it looks to me? Do I take my joy from knowing this, or do I tend to draw my contentment from pleasant situations and circumstances?

Peace

Do I bring a calming effect to every situation, or do I stir up people's feathers? Am I a reconciler or an instigator? Do I tend to fix the blame or fix the problem?

Patience

Do I give people room to fail, and then help them look for the lessons of life that can be extracted from that failure? Or do I keep score of hits and errors?

Kindness

Am I kind? When working with people under my supervision or care, do I appeal to them kindly? Or do I have a tendency to order them around? How do I behave toward my family?

Goodness

Is the core of my heart good? Do I want the success of others, or do I look out only for myself, regardless of what happens to others?

Faithfulness

Am I loyal? Can I keep confidences, or do I have the tendency to share private information about others? Am I a faithful spouse, or do I emotionally court other relationships?

Gentleness

How do I deal with others' failures, especially if it affects me? Am I more concerned about my welfare or theirs?

Self-control

Do I control my thoughts or do they stray? Am I able to discipline my emotions and sexual desires?

Take the time to practice these character qualities God is wanting to build in you and express through you. The more you practice these things, the more fruitful you'll be in your attitude, business, ministry and family. So *practice, practice, practice!*

CHAPTER SEVEN

NEVER GIVE UP!

Never, never, never give up!

WINSTON CHURCHILL

Let's all agree on one thing: Every one of us will have the dubious honor of being on the receiving end of life's setbacks—frequently. We all experience speed bumps in life. Suffering is inevitable, but misery is an option. Suffering will change you, but not necessarily for the better. You have to *choose* to change for the better.

You can let your setbacks become stumbling blocks or make them stepping-stones. Life can make you bitter or better. The choice is yours. Remember the saying we reflected upon earlier: "Ten percent of life is what happens to you—the other 90 percent is how you respond to what happens to you."

ALL OF US HAVE STUMBLED, BUT GOD IS NOT DONE WITH US. HE BELIEVES IN US. THE GAME IS NOT OVER YET!

One of my favorite Scriptures is Proverbs 24:16. It has given me renewed hope through the years. The passage reads, "For a righteous man falls seven times, and rises again, but the wicked stumble in time of calamity."

I like that. You see, failure is not something that happens when you fall down. Failure is when you refuse to get up again! Some people get knocked down, and although they stand up, you can tell they've remained down on the inside where it counts.

Pull your spirit up again! Set your sights back on God's purposes for you. The game is not over. You can do so much more! *He* is able, even when you are not!

David stumbled but got back up, and God made him Israel's greatest king. Jacob stumbled but got back up and became the father of the 12 tribes of Israel. Paul attempted to annihilate the Christians, but God took hold of his life and used him to take the gospel to the Gentiles. Peter denied the Lord in His time of greatest need. Yet Peter got back up and shook off the shame, and God used him mightily to spread His message of life to the known world.

THE GAME IS NOT OVER YET

A famous story is told of the 1929 Rose Bowl, in which the Yellow Jackets of Georgia Tech played the California Golden Bears, and a young man by the name of Roy Riegels learned a valuable lesson in the game of life.

Late in the first half, Georgia Tech running back Stumpy Thomason fumbled, and after a brief but furious skirmish, Cal lineman Roy Riegels recovered the football and dashed toward the end zone, determined to score.

Only one problem: He was headed for the wrong goal line!

Benny Lom, one of his own teammates, took off in hot pursuit of the wrong-way Riegels. Lom finally caught up with Riegels and tackled him on Cal's own three-yard line. On the next play, a desperation California punt was blocked in the end zone for a safety. Those two points would prove to be the margin by which they would lose the game.

At halftime, the Cal team gathered in the locker room. No one said a word. Finally, Coach Nibbs Price spoke up. "Okay. The same guys that came out in the first half will start the second." The players headed for the field—all except Roy Riegels. He sat still on the bench, his face buried in his hands.

"You heard me, Roy," said Coach Price. "I said the same team that came out of the first half will start the second. And that includes you!"

"I can't go out there again, Coach. I can't face my teammates. I've let you down, shamed our team and embarrassed our school. I can't go out there."

Coach Price straightened him up, looked him in the eyes and said, "The game's only half over, Riegels. Get out there and make something of yourself. The game's only half over!"

The Georgia Tech players later said they had never seen anyone play with the determination and intensity that Riegels showed in the second half of the 1929 Rose Bowl game.

When I recall that story, I think to myself, *What a great coach that Nibbs Price was!* And when I think of our Lord and the way He believes in each of us, I think, *What a great Lord we serve!*

All of us have stumbled, and many of us have often run the wrong way. But God is not done with us. Granted, there will be a few fumbles and misguided moves on the fields of our lives. Still, He prods us back into the game. He believes in us. The game is not over yet!

THE ISSUE IS LOVE, NOT PERFORMANCE

Peter had a history of fumbles and errors, but his biggest mistake came on the last night of Jesus' life—only hours after Peter had sworn eternal loyalty to the Lord. When Jesus was arrested in the Garden of Gethsemane, Peter fled. That same night, as Jesus was on trial, Peter denied Him not once but three times. A few hours later, Jesus was crucified and buried.

I'll bet Peter blamed himself for Jesus' death. I can just hear him: "If only I had stopped Judas, none of this would have happened. Some leader I am! I couldn't even stand up to a servant girl who recognized me as His disciple. What a failure!"

Peter felt so disqualified from ministry that he traded in his shepherd's staff for a fishing pole and headed back to the lake. Although he knew God had called him to ministry, his recent failures drove him away from that calling.

Then the whole story changes. As Peter and his friends returned from a terrible night of fishing, Jesus stood on the edge of the lake and called to the disciples. When Peter recognized it was the resurrected Lord, he left the others behind and swam to shore. There he sat face to face with the One he had so completely failed.

I've stood at the spot on the northern shore of Galilee where this meeting took place. A plaque there depicts the event. I remember being overwhelmed with emotion as a few of us stood there recalling the meeting between Jesus and Peter. I guess I felt overwhelmed, because so often I feel as though I, too, have failed. Peter's denial seems a minor offense compared to the times when I have turned my back on the Lord. How many times I have denied Him, refused to identify with Him and instead blended in with the crowd!

Yet I can hear Him speak to my heart just as He addressed Peter:

> When they had finished breakfast, Jesus said to Simon Peter, "Simon, son of John, do you love Me more than these?" He said to Him, "Yes, Lord; You know that I love You." He said to him, "Tend My lambs." He said to him again a second time, "Simon, son of John, do you love Me?" He said to Him, "Yes, Lord; You know that I love You." He said to him, "Shepherd My sheep." He said to him the third time, "Simon, son of John, do you love Me?" Peter was grieved because He said to him the third time, "Do you love Me?" And he said to Him, "Lord, You know all things; You know that I love You." Jesus said to him, "Tend My sheep" (John 21:15-17).

I am always amazed at the answers of the Lord. If I had been confronting Peter, I would have yelled at him, "You creep! Why did you leave me in the lurch like that? Great friend you are!" I would have confronted his poor performance.

But Jesus didn't confront his performance. He confronted his heart.

"Peter, do you love Me?"

"Yes, Lord. I do love You."

"Good. Then get back in the game. It's not over yet!"

The prerequisite for restoration is not performance; it is love. Love will always be God's highest test. Don't put a magnifying glass on your failure. Put your magnifying glass on love, and it will help you see things the way Jesus does. That's always the best way to look at things anyway!

STAY THE COURSE

One of the most powerful ingredients for developing staying power, or the ability to get back in the game and stay there, is stubbornness. That's right. You can be stubborn in a right way. I guess you could call it endurance, but I like to call it stubbornness.

Of course, you can be stubborn in the wrong way, too. That could be termed being stiff-necked or obstinate. But that's not what I am talking about.

Stubborn obedience to the call of God on my life helps me get through the gauntlet of critics and survive the nagging memories of past mistakes. I know God has called me to represent Him during my stay in this world. (He has called you to do the same!) Come what may, I must finish the course. I must run the race with endurance—stubborn endurance, mind you—until He takes me home to be with Him forever.

I guess we're in pretty good company, because it was prophesied of Jesus that He would stay the course, too, no matter what came His way:

He will not be disheartened or crushed, until He has established justice in the earth (Isa. 42:4).

He had made a choice. He would not be disheartened or crushed until His assignment was through! He made a choice, and I get to do the same.

We will have many opportunities to bail out along the way. There will be plenty of reasons to resign. I've experienced many! No one ever needs to look far for a reason to get divorced or to leave a home church. There will always be plenty of justification to have an affair. There will always be plenty of sorrows to drown in beer at the local bar.

MAKE THE CHOICE
TO STAY
THE COURSE.

What will give you longevity is not the absence of stress or trials. Look at Jesus' life. It was riddled with problems. People trying to betray Him, demon-possessed people trying to grab onto Him, sick people lining up to touch Him and Pharisees constantly testing Him. Yet He refused to be disheartened or crushed!

Make the same choice to stay the course. Sure, there may be many course corrections along the way. Maybe even a few deviations from the original flight plan, but *stay the course!*

THE SHORTEST SPEECH NEVER TO BE FORGOTTEN

Sir Winston Churchill was once asked to address his alma mater in a commencement speech. He had become quite a legend by this time due to his courage and confidence during World War II.

The auditorium was overflowing with graduating students, parents, dignitaries and guests. He arrived with his classic top hat, coat, stogie and cane. After an introduction, including a long litany of his accomplishments, he slowly made his way to the podium.

Looking over the students, an intensity came over his countenance. He leaned forward and gave the shortest speech those students ever received.

With a tone that reflected the character of both warrior and diplomat, he said, "Never, never, never give up!" Taking a deep breath, he repeated with greater volume, "Never! Never! Never give up!" He turned, put on his top hat and coat, took up his cane, picked up his stogie and left.

We'll all be faced with battles, and when the battles are over, the critics will begin. But nevah give up! You'll want to, no doubt. But the only way the devil can defeat you is if you give him permission to do so. Don't you do it! The game's not over until God says it is!

The following is a poem written by Kent Keith. It is so appropriate!

ANYWAY
People are unreasonable,
    illogical, self-centered.
Love them ANYWAY.

If you do good, people will accuse you
of selfish, ulterior motives.
Do good ANYWAY.
If you are successful, you'll win
false friends and make true enemies.
Succeed ANYWAY.
Honesty and kindness may
make you vulnerable.
Be honest and kind ANYWAY.
The good you do today
may very well be forgotten tomorrow.
But do good ANYWAY.
The biggest people with the
biggest ideas can get shot down
by the smallest people
with the smallest minds.
But think big ANYWAY.
Give the world the best you got.
You may very well get kicked
in the teeth for it.
But give the world the best you got . . . ANYWAY.

CHAPTER EIGHT

FINISH WELL

So teach us to number our days, that we may

present to Thee a heart of wisdom.

PSALM 90:12

We have only one life to live for Jesus on this earth, and it will soon be over.

As I grow older, I am increasingly amazed how quickly time passes. It's like the rewinding of a videotape: The closer it gets to home, the faster it goes! So it is with each of us.

What if someone came to you and offered to deposit $86,400 into your bank account every morning? Wouldn't that be heavenly! There's only one catch: You must wisely spend or invest the entire amount every day. Any squandering of the money is not acceptable. Nothing can be carried over, and anything left in the account will be lost to you at midnight. Of course, another $86,400 will be deposited the following morning.

What would you do in this situation? You bet! You would be sure to spend all of the money or invest it wisely.

Well, this happens to you every day. Only the gift is not measured in dollars and cents; it is measured in time. You are given 86,400 seconds every day. How you use them is up to you. You can squander the time and lose its benefit, or you can invest it wisely and be rewarded.

Don't live a squandered life. Since you have only one life to give, live it well!

What separates a futile life from a fruitful one? Your attitude. Your attitude will be the difference between existing and living!

TAKE A LOOK AT YOUR TWO MOST VALUABLE DECISIONS

Let me pause here to ask you again to evaluate the two most important decisions in your life.

Your most important life decision will be your choice of whether or not to follow Jesus Christ. Your choice to open your heart to Him will be the most eternal decision you will ever make. If you have not done that, don't hesitate for another moment! There is no greater choice than to choose Him to be Lord in your life, no matter how many possessions you own, how much money you have made or how much power you have accumulated.

Jesus reminds us, "How do you benefit if you gain the whole world but lose your own soul in the process?" (Mark 8:36, *NLT*).

Now, as a Christian, let me reveal your second most important decision in this life: choosing the attitude with which you will follow Christ. The first decision will determine how *eternal* your life will be. The second will determine how *effective* your life will be!

Just because you are a Christian does not guarantee fruitfulness. I have often met Christians with poor attitudes that sour their relationships, families, ministry and potential for success. This need not be so!

Anyone can develop an attitude that attracts success.

SEIZE THE DAY!

In the motion picture *Dead Poets Society*, Robin Williams plays the part of John Keating, an iconoclastic instructor hired to teach English literature at a buttoned-down, straightlaced, all-boys prep school. Determined to interest the boys in what they believe to be a boring subject, Keating employs a highly unorthodox teaching style. On the first day of class, with an impish smile, he walks out of the classroom and implores the boys to follow him.

In the hallway, Keating gathers the boys around a glass trophy case containing dusty trophies, school memorabilia and some aging black-and-white photographs of students from long, long ago. There Keating asks one of the students to open his textbook and recite from the poem "To the Virgins to Make Much of Time." The boy hesitantly reads aloud:

> Gather ye rosebuds while ye may,
> Old Time is still a-flying;
> And this same flower that smiles today,
> Tomorrow will be dying.

"Gather ye rosebuds while ye may," Keating repeats. "The Latin term for that sentiment is *carpe diem*. Now who knows what that means?"

The know-it-all boy of the group volunteers, "Seize the day."

"Seize the day," says Keating. "Gather ye rosebuds while ye may. Why does the poet use these lines?"

Another boy takes a shot. "Because he was in a hurry?"

Imitating the sound of a game-show buzzer, the teacher corrects him. "No, but thank you for playing." He then turns to the boys and explains, "Because *we are all food for worms*, lads! Because, believe it or not, one day each and every one of us in this room is going to stop breathing, turn cold and die!"

TEACH US TO NUMBER OUR DAYS, THAT WE MAY PRESENT TO THEE A HEART OF WISDOM.

PSALMS 90:12

Keating calls the boys' attention to the trophy case. "Now I would like you to step forward over here and peruse some of the faces from the past. You've walked past them many times, but I don't think you've really looked at them."

The boys stare blankly at the photos.

"They're not that different from you, are they?" the teacher suggests. "Same haircuts. Full of hormones, just like you. Invincible, just like you feel. The world is their oyster! They believe they're destined for great things, just like many of you. Their eyes are full of hope, just like you."

Keating pauses to let this sink in.

"Did they wait until it was too late to make from their lives even one iota of what they were capable? Because, you see gentlemen, these boys are now fertilizing daffodils." Keating smiles. "But if you listen real close, you can hear them whisper their legacy to you. Go on, lean in."

The boys crane their necks toward the trophy case.

"Hear it?" Then, as if interpreting for the souls of these past alumni, Keating whispers in a hoarse voice, intoned with a sense of deep urgency, "Carpe diem. Seize the day, boys! Make your lives extraordinary!"

Jesus said it this way:

> You're here to be light, bringing out the God-colors in the world. God is not a secret to be kept. We're going public with this, as public as a city on a hill (Matt. 5:14, *THE MESSAGE*).

Carpe diem! Seize the day and bring out the God-colors in your world. Within you lies the Holy Spirit, infused through your being by the breath of God. Don't keep it a secret. Begin to live your God-given call by shining your light through your life.

You don't have to be a world-famous evangelist to shine. Just start by shining your light to those around you every day. And what is the beacon through which your light will shine to those around you? Your extraordinary attitude!

FOLLOW THE FOUR KEYS TO BUILDING AN EXTRAORDINARY ATTITUDE

Each of us can live an extraordinary life with an attitude of excellence, but it must be diligently cultivated. Let's take a look at four keys to living an extraordinary life.

1. Aim for the Right Target

What are you shooting for in life? What is your goal? If you could identify only one thing that drives your life, what would it be?

In the movie *City Slickers*, three friends from New York vacation together at a dude ranch out West, where they will learn to rope, ride and herd cattle. Their foreman on the climactic cattle drive is a real-life cowboy by the name of Curly, a wizened loner and the last of a dying breed.

One day, as they're poking along on the range, Curly talks with Mitch, a middle-aged radio advertising salesman who has become disenchanted with his life at work and at home.

"A cowboy leads a different kind of life," intones the crusty Curly. "When there *were* cowboys. They're a dying breed. Still means something to me, though. In a couple of days, we'll move this herd across the river, drive them through the valley. Ahhh," he laughs softly, "there's nothing like bringing in the herd."

"You see, now that's great," chirps the less-than-rustic Mitch. "Your life makes sense to you."

Curly laughs heartily, and Mitch just looks confused. At this point the worldly wise Curly cuts to the core of this middle-aged businessman's trip. "You all come out here about the same age. Same problems. Spend 50 weeks a year getting knots in your rope. Then you think two weeks up here will untie them for you. None of you get it."

The two men fall silent under the weight of these words.

Curly continues, "Do you know what the secret of life is?"

"No, what?"

Curly raises his weathered hand and seems to point skyward. "This."

"Your finger?"

Still pointing, Curly says, "One thing. Just one thing. You stick to that."

"That's great, but what's the one thing?" prods Mitch eagerly, asking on behalf of us all.

Curly leans in and says, "That's what *you've* got to figure out."

If you could point to just one thing undergirding your life, what would that be? What would you choose to focus on, to make your first priority and your ultimate goal?

Take a look at the list below and decide.

- Money
- Fame
- Prestige
- Power
- Notoriety
- Being the best
- Sports/recreation
- Financial independence/security
- Success in business or ministry
- Family
- Peace
- Jesus

For many years my choice was Jesus. But for some reason, without my realizing it, He had slipped from my top spot. I had been vacillating unknowingly for a few years. I was driven more by the fear that I would not have enough money saved for retirement, and it skewed my perspective on life. I struggled with periodic pangs of anxiety, and I was easily distracted as I tried to make the right investments for my future, constantly watching the stock market fluctuate.

EVERYTHING DEPENDS ON WHAT YOU ARE SHOOTING FOR. WHEN WE AIM AT THE WRONG TARGET, LIFE ITSELF BECOMES ELUSIVE.

Then I revisited my list. My perspective returned only when I resolved to return to my first love, my true goal in life—Jesus. When my perspective was firmly in place, so was my heart for what God had called me to do.

Everything depends on what you are shooting for. When we aim at the wrong target, life itself becomes elusive. Be sure that you are aiming at the right target. Keep your perspective clearly focused on that target, and frequently double-check to make sure that it's the right target.

Take some time out right now. Stop rowing through life so frantically and check to see if you are still headed in the right direction!

What's your one thing?

The Special Olympics is a wonderful organization that encourages children and adults with special learning needs or physical handicaps to compete in athletic events. Their track and field events are often exhilarating opportunities to be surprised by the most unpretentious and authentic expressions of life.

It happened in one of the sprints. Young children between the ages of 8 and 12 had gathered at the starting line. Some were in wheelchairs, some were in braces, and all were filled with anticipation! Parents and relatives packed the stands, each cheering his or her own child on with an exuberance that would make the fans' zeal at a World Series game pale in comparison.

The starter fired his pistol into the air. They were off! The supreme effort of each child touched the heart of everyone present. There were children with crutches, laboring to control their limbs. Kids with Down's syndrome ran alongside those with leg braces.

One child in a wheelchair had turned her chair around, moving in reverse with her little feet motoring along to give her more speed. Soon, however, she began to veer off course, and it wasn't long before she ended up lodged against the grandstands. Unable to free herself from this predicament, she began to call out for help. A handicapped boy and another with Down's syndrome heard her pleas. They ran to where she was, turned her chair around and began pushing her toward the finish. Amid shouts of jubilation and victory, the little retrieval group crossed the finish line together.

Their objective was not necessarily to finish first. You see, they thought their goal was to see that everyone made it across the line, and that required the help of every child involved.

What has God asked you to do with your life? If you were to write a one-paragraph personal mission statement, how would it read? If you're not sure what your life's assignment is, then how will you know which opportunities to accept and which ones to reject? As the Cheshire Cat pointed out to Alice, if you don't know where you're going, *any* road will get you there.

Feeling my focus was diffused, I sat down and hammered out what I felt was God's direction and assignment for my life. Upon this statement would hang all the activities of my ministry. It would help me to decide which activities I would say yes to and which I would say no to. This statement would act as an internal homing device to guide me in the race that was set before me.

Here is that statement:

> To model and communicate biblical truths in such a way as to inspire character, equip leaders, heighten the awareness of Jesus Christ and effectively evangelize those whom God is drawing to Himself.

Where is your road taking you? Do you know where you want to end up? If you know these things, then you're well on your way to success. If you don't, then take a few moments, perhaps even a few days, to pound out your personal mission statement. Answer this life-changing question: *What has God asked me to do with my life?*

An attitude that attracts success begins with knowing which opportunities to accept and which to reject. This way you will begin to develop not just an existence but a life that is about answering God's call every single day.

Remember, first aim for the right target. What are you aiming for? What is your goal? That will determine the race you run.

2. Run the Right Race

God sets a different race before each and every one of us. You cannot run someone else's race; you can only run your own.

> Therefore, since we have so great a cloud of witnesses surrounding us, let us also lay aside every encumbrance, and the sin which so easily entangles us, and let us run with endurance *the race that is set before us* (Heb. 12:1, emphasis mine).

If you run the wrong race, you'll end up at the wrong finish line.

In my book *Doing Church as a Team*, I tell the true story of an Olympic marathon runner who, although he clearly outran the field, was disqualified from medal contention. Why? Because in his fatigue and confusion, he had crossed the wrong finish line!

Sometimes we, as Christians, can live discontented lives because we are running toward the wrong finish lines. We put in a Herculean effort, but we aren't investing our time and resources where God wants us to invest. Instead, we have our own desires and we try to use God to help us get where we want to go. Like summoning the genie from a magic lamp, we try to rub God the right way, so He will answer our prayers the way we want them answered. We don't want to wait for counsel, so we ask God to bless what we're doing rather than to help us do what He's blessing.

Try praying this prayer. It will change your perspective and help you to stay on track and finish well:

> *Lord, here is my life. Use my life for Your purposes and*
> *Your desires. Lord, come live Your life through me.*
> *Whatever I have, whatever skills I may possess, whatever my*
> *abilities and capabilities, finances or treasures, Lord, I lay them*
> *at Your feet. How can You use them? You instruct me, so I can*
> *be a faithful steward and use my life for Your purposes.*
> *Whether I have much or little, I will be content because*
> *I know You are using my life for Your purposes.*
> *Come, Lord, live Your life through me.*

Instead of telling God what you will do for Him, ask Him to do *His* work through you! Instead of telling God how you plan to live for Him, ask Him what His plans are for your life. By doing this, you will tap into His power to fulfill His plans His way! There's no greater satisfaction than when you are experiencing the surge of His life through your soul.

"For I know the plans that I have for you," declares the LORD, "plans for welfare and not for calamity to give you a future and a hope" (Jer. 29:11).

3. Understand What Satisfies Your Soul
Jesus gives us the secret of contentment:

> Do not be anxious then, saying, "What shall we eat?" or "What shall we drink?" or "With what shall we clothe ourselves?" . . . for your heavenly Father knows that you need all these things. But seek first His kingdom and His righteousness; and all these things shall be added to you (Matt. 6:31-33).

Contentment cannot be acquired directly. Rather, it is a by-product of a life that is focused on the right things. Truly content people are those whose aim in life is something much bigger than attaining mere contentment alone.

If your sole aim is to acquire possessions and money in order to be comfortable and content, then contentment will be as elusive as a butterfly.

A few years ago, the whole world had its eyes on an American billionaire who desired to fly the fastest plane in the world. So he designed, built and piloted the world's fastest airplane. He wanted to have boats and condos and live in exotic places, so he bought them. He amassed such a great fortune that he was said to have had two U.S. presidents at his bidding. He believed he could gain contentment by having more affairs and sexual endeavors, by going on more expeditions, explorations and excursions. And so he did.

Let's fast forward the tape to the end of his life. His hair is long and unkempt, his beard disheveled, and his arms are covered with the puncture marks of a drug addict frantically attempting to jab contentment into his veins. His fingernails are long and unruly, resembling pale yellow corkscrews. Bedridden, he sits in a drug-induced trance, peering at life through dark, sunken eye sockets in an emaciated body. He has missed life itself.

LEARN TO UNDERSTAND WHAT SATISFIES YOUR SOUL; OTHERWISE, YOU WILL NEVER DEVELOP AN ATTITUDE OF TRUE CONTENTMENT.

He lives in self-imposed solitary confinement. He is a man who spent the best years of his life desperately searching for contentment but never finding it. He finally dies in a lonely pit of despair.

I am sure you will recognize this man's name: Howard Hughes. He lived his whole life hoping to find contentment but came up empty-handed. He traded his soul for possessions and lost it all in the home stretch.

Read what Jesus had to say about a rich man's foolish pursuits:

"I will say to my soul, 'Soul, you have many goods laid up for many years to come; take your ease, eat, drink and be merry.'" But God said to him, "You fool! This very night your soul is required of you; and now who will own what you have prepared?" So is the man who lays up treasure for himself, and is not rich toward God (Luke 12:19-21).

Humorist and television talk-show host Johnny Carson made millions of dollars from his late-night program, "The Tonight Show." With all his fortune, his candor and colorful jokes, you might think he would be one of the happiest people around. But in an interview, one of his relatives reported, "Johnny is one of the saddest people I know. He's someone who's always looking for a good time, but never finding it."

Learn to understand what truly satisfies you—what satisfies your soul. Otherwise, you will never develop an attitude of true contentment. You'll always be looking for a good time but never finding it.

4. Make Contentment an Inside Job

The apostle Paul did not live a cushioned, aristocratic life, but he developed a world-class attitude that carried him through every storm.

> I have learned to be content in whatever circumstances I am. I know how to get along with humble means, and I also know how to live in prosperity; in any and every circumstance I have learned the secret of being filled and going hungry, both of having abundance and suffering need (Phil. 4:11-12).

Paul had been hungry. He had been abandoned. He had been stoned, shipwrecked, whipped, beaten and left for dead. Paul had been mocked, ridiculed and slandered. When he wrote these words about contentment, he was writing them from prison. He knew that within a few years he would be tortured to death. How in the world was he able to maintain a godly attitude under such circumstances? How could he possibly say he knew what it meant to be content?

Because his aim in life was much bigger than contentment itself. Paul's aim was not to attain a lifestyle of convenience and comfort. Paul's aim was to know God and to serve Him with all his heart. His sole desire was that his life would somehow, in some way, be used to bring God's purposes to pass. He sought first the kingdom of God by offering up his skills and his influence so the Lord could use them. Then contentment flooded his life, and his attitude turned his prison cell into the place where nearly half the New Testament would be written!

Contentment is vital in developing an extraordinary attitude. It's the final and critical key in your process. Each of these four keys seems simple, but each is eternally priceless.

Remember, start off right by aiming for the right target, the one God has for you as you "run your particular race to win" (see Heb. 12:1).

The next step is to just do it! Run the right race.

The last two go hand in hand. Understand what satisfies your soul, and do so by learning contentment.

With these keys in hand, you'll be able to run your race *and* finish well!

CHAPTER NINE

GO BACK TO THE SOURCE

Have this attitude in yourselves which was also in Christ Jesus.

PHILIPPIANS 2:5

During a class on American history, some second graders were asked, "Can you name the foreigner who was a big help to the American colonists during the Revolutionary War?" One boy quickly raised his hand and when called upon, confidently answered, "God!"

YOUR ATTITUDE, IN ESSENCE, IS THE EXPRESSION OF YOUR FAITH AND THE DISPLAY OF YOUR CHARACTER.

The bottom line of developing an attitude that attracts success is not simply found in positive thinking. Don't get me wrong. There's nothing wrong with positive thinking. When you consider the alternative, negative thinking is no option!

However, we must go far beyond a positive outlook. E. Stanley Jones once said, "Anything less than God will let you down." Jesus said, "Apart from Me you can do nothing" (John 15:5). We desperately need His help, and if we ask Him, He will never turn us down:

Ask and it will be given to you; seek and you will find; knock and the door will be opened to you (Matt. 7:7, *NIV*).

God is the only one I know who can change the human heart. The government can't, money won't and ideal circumstances don't. Without God, our efforts will be futile at best.

Unless the LORD builds the house, its builders labor in vain (Ps. 127:1, *NIV*).

Developing a world-class attitude takes decisiveness, commitment, perseverance and a willingness to be effective at this thing called life. Your attitude is, in essence, the expression of your faith and the display of your character. It is not simply the result of positive thinking. It is the result of Jesus Christ's working in your life moment to moment and your cooperation with His instructions.

THE BIBLE IS YOUR ATTITUDE INSTRUCTION MANUAL

The Bible is the greatest book ever written on the subject of life. You cannot find a better book on leadership, business, money, family or marriage. When God's Word fills your minds, you can't help but develop a better attitude! And when His instructions and counsel begin to find their way into your conversation, relationships and habits, then your attitude will be transformed.

We all will have two teachers in life: the teacher of wisdom and the teacher of consequences. Both are tremendous teachers, and you will learn from both. There is a price to be paid to enroll in each class. However, the price that must be paid for the teaching of consequences can cost you everything you have. For some, it has cost them years; others have paid with their futures, and for still others, it has cost them their families. You will no doubt learn from consequences, but she can be a cruel taskmaster.

Wisdom, on the other hand, comes from lessons learned vicariously through others' consequences. You can learn from others' experiences without having to go through the pain yourself. But there is a price for obtaining wisdom as well, because wisdom requires you to develop something called discipline. When you would rather get angry than be patient, discipline is painful! When you want to tell someone off but you know it would be wiser to let it go, this also can be painful.

Be aware that the pain of discipline will cost you pennies, whereas the pain of regret can cost you millions.

Making Wisdom a Sport

I follow a principle found in Proverbs 10:23: "Doing wickedness is like sport to a fool; and so is wisdom to a man of understanding." The man of understanding makes a sport of doing what is wise.

What an interesting idea! I love sports and can be fairly competitive, so this passage is speaking my language! The Bible gives me permission to train for and inaugurate a new sport—the sport of wisdom.

Here's how this works in my life. When I come to an impasse or am presented with a problem, the game begins. Others in this situation tend to bail out immediately, saying, "It can't be done; it's impossible!" I hear that all the time; but in actuality, these people have only succeeded in disqualifying themselves. I say, let the games begin!

First, I try to figure out what would be the wisest thing to do in this problematic situation. Sounds tough? Here's the great thing about this sport: You can get help, counsel or advice from anyone—and it's not cheating! You can recruit great thinkers and problem solvers, and you can consult any book to get fresh answers and new ways of looking at the problem. But remember, your goal is to solve the problem in the wisest way possible.

So I ask God for wisdom. James 1:5 says, "But if any of you lacks wisdom, let him ask of God, who gives to all men generously and without reproach, and it will be given to him." Pretty good deal!

Solomon asked God for wisdom, and it so pleased God that He gave Solomon much, much more than what he had asked for:

And God said to him, "Because you have asked this thing and have not asked for yourself long life, nor have asked riches for yourself, nor have you asked for the life of your enemies, but have asked for yourself discernment to understand justice, behold, I have done according to your words. Behold, I have given you a wise and discerning heart, so that there has been no one like you before you, nor shall one like you arise after you. And I have also given you what you have not asked, both riches and honor, so that there will not be any among the kings like you all your days" (1 Kings 3:11-13).

This approach to life has helped me more than you can know. I'm still a beginner at this sport. But with a little more practice, I hope to keep advancing.

Finding the Source of Wisdom Training

Wisdom can come from many different sources. We can learn a great deal by experiencing every new thing firsthand and feeling pangs of consequences, but that may not be the best way. Experience can be a good teacher, but wisdom is far more desirable. Why?

THY WORD IS A LAMP TO MY FEET,

AND A LIGHT TO MY PATH.

PSALMS 119:105

What if we could gather the greatest 400 leaders of all time and enlist them as our personal teachers and mentors. Sound great? Yet even a year with them wouldn't be enough to gain the wisdom we are searching for. So what if we took the accounts of the lives of these great men and women and recorded them in a book? Better yet, what if their experiences were edited so only the most profound and critical lessons were recorded, ones that would be most useful to us. How much would you pay for a book like this? Would you pay hundreds, even thousands of dollars for this treasure? But wait!

God has compiled one of these amazing books for you. And I'm guessing you already own one or more copies! It is called the Bible.

In this fantastic book you will find the best of the best—their lives, their loves, their triumphs, their failures and their testimonies of faith. And God has edited their stories so we can read all about their experiences and the consequences of their actions. Instead of having to go through what they did, we are able to deposit the gems of what they learned into our hearts—and our lives are transformed!

All Scripture is inspired by God and profitable for teaching, for reproof, for correction, for training in righteousness; that the man of God may be adequate, equipped for every good work (2 Tim. 3:16-17).

David wrote, "I have more understanding than all my teachers, for Your testimonies are my meditation" (Ps. 119:99, *NKJV*). In other words, the instructions of God's Word gave David wisdom beyond his years—and it will do the same for you. His Word will be the ageless mentor to help you be "conformed to the image of His Son" (Rom. 8:29).

Make a habit of reading the Bible on a daily basis. Each day you will receive another gem that God will tuck into your heart. As you hide His Word deep inside, you'll begin to see in yourself a day-to-day transformation, an ever-increasing resemblance to Jesus.

"Your word I have hidden in my heart, that I might not sin against You!" (Ps. 119:11, *NKJV*). The mistakes you commonly made in the past will become more infrequent as you allow the Holy Spirit to guide your words and actions. The Bible is one of God's best tools for helping you to develop an attitude that attracts success!

PRAYER IS THE TIME FOR MAKING AN ATTITUDE ADJUSTMENT

Prayer is one of the more elusive exercises in a Christian's life. It's a bit like watering a plant: You may not see immediate results, but if the discipline of prayer is neglected, the consequences can be disastrous. Prayer must be a habit—a daily habit.

When you take the time to pray through your upcoming decisions and plans, you are learning how to think deeply in the presence of God. He helps you by His Spirit and gives you wisdom and insight. Keep a journal near you when you are praying to jot down instructions and understanding that the Lord reveals to you. I often fill my own journal with page after page of what God is telling me about my attitude, my faith, my perspective and my behavior.

Remember, however, that prayer is not simply a venue to complain before God. Often we misuse prayer and use God to try and get our own agendas accomplished. Listen to what Paul says: "Devote yourselves to prayer, keeping alert in it with an attitude of thanksgiving" (Col. 4:2). Our attitude in prayer is important! We are to approach God with an attitude of thanksgiving.

Billy Graham once gave a short illustration of the effect prayer should have on us. He was watching a ship pull into dock. Thick ropes were fastened to the dock, and he heard the huge engines of the ship begin to whir. Then he noticed something intriguing: As the ropes drew taut, the dock wasn't drawn to the ship; rather the ship was drawn to the dock!

Prayer should be exactly like that. When we pray, we don't pull God down to our level in order for Him to accomplish what we've got assigned for Him to do. Instead, prayer draws us near to God in order that we receive His strength to do His bidding! How often we forget God doesn't exist for our purposes. We exist for *His*.

It is through prayer that God reveals simple but key truths that help us to see things from a whole new vantage point. When you ask to see things His way, you can't help but have your attitude changed!

And in the same way—by our faith—the Holy Spirit helps us with our daily problems and in our praying. For we don't even know what we should pray for, nor how to pray as we should; but the Holy Spirit prays for us (Rom. 8:26, *TLB*).

Now You Get To Choose!

I call heaven and earth to witness against you today, that I have set before you life and death, the blessing and the curse. So choose life in order that you may live, you and your descendants (Deut. 30:19).

Moses told God's people they had to make a choice between life and death. One would bring a curse, and the other would result in life.

Developing an attitude that attracts success is a choice. Let me remind you again: The most important decision you will ever make in life is your decision to follow Jesus Christ. This decision will determine the *eternity* of your life.

The second most important decision you'll make will be the attitude with which you will follow the Lord. This decision will determine the *quality* of your life.

THE MOST IMPORTANT DECISION YOU WILL EVER MAKE IN LIFE IS YOUR DECISION TO FOLLOW JESUS CHRIST.

The story is told of two prisoners lying on their bunks one evening. The prisoner on the top bunk was staring out the window of his cell into the night sky. The stars were spread out in a splendid array, with an occasional shooting star making the evening sky a spectacular display of divine fireworks.

Calling to his cell mate in the bunk below, the man said, "Hey, wake up! Look at the stars! They're beautiful. Look!"

"Aw, leave me alone," his cell mate grunted.

"Come on. Just look. The stars tonight are the brightest I've ever seen!"

His cell mate groaned and turned over in his bunk to look out at the night sky. After a brief glance, he growled, "I don't see no stars. All I see are the bars."

One prisoner saw the stars; the other saw the bars. It all depends on your attitude, doesn't it? Contentment is an inside job. You will either be a master or a victim of your attitude.

So, too, God sets before you the decision of serving Him either with a great attitude or with a poor one. Choose a good one that you might experience life! Yes, life for you and your descendants!

But it takes training, discipline and desire to develop your perspective to see what's good. Choose, because both will be present—the stars and the bars. Look for the stars, and you can reach them! Look for the bars, and they'll surely imprison you.

Look for the stars. They're out tonight. Follow them. They just may lead you to a bright future.

You're only one attitude away from a fantastic life!

Wayne Cordeiro is senior pastor of New Hope Christian Fellowship in Oahu, a new work that was planted in September 1995. Within five years, attendance at their weekend services had grown to more than 7,000, making New Hope Oahu one of the fastest-growing churches in America. More than 5,200 people received Christ for the first time during these first years of the church.

Pastor Wayne has also planted more than 20 other churches in Hawaii, Guam, Samoa, Finland and Japan. Prior to moving to Oahu, he was senior pastor at New Hope Christian Fellowship in Hilo, Hawaii, for almost 12 years. Under his pastoral leadership, the New Hope Hilo congregation grew from 50 to over 1,700 and launched a new 20-acre church facility, The Gathering Place.

Wayne was raised in Palolo Valley on Oahu, and he lived in Japan for three years. He then moved to Oregon where he finished his schooling and ministry training during the next 12 years. He served with Youth For Christ for seven years and as a staff pastor for three years at Faith Center Foursquare Church in Eugene, Oregon, before returning to Hawaii.

He is an accomplished songwriter and performer who has released six albums. Pastor Wayne's teaching radio program, "Words of New Hope," airs on KAIM and KUMU in Hawaii. As president of the Pacific Rim Bible Institute, he is working to train, develop and support emerging leaders who will plant twenty-first-century churches in the Pacific Rim.

Pastor Wayne travels extensively throughout the islands, the continental United States and Asia to speak at conferences, churches, civic gatherings, prisons, high school assemblies, business forums and leadership conventions. He also speaks to businesses, companies and corporations about restructuring and growth strategies.

He has written three other books: *Doing Church as a Team, Gems Along the Way* and the forthcoming Regal book *The Dream Releasers.*

Pastor Wayne and his wife, Anna, have three children, Amy, Aaron and Abigail.

For more information about resources by Wayne Cordeiro or to inquire about speaking engagements, please write or call:

New Hope Christian Fellowship Oahu
290 Sand Island Road
Honolulu, Hawaii 96819
Phone (808) 842-4242
Fax (808) 842-4241
www.eNewHope.org

We would love to hear from you!

Please share with us
how this book has helped or blessed you.

For your comments and suggestions:

email us at   Inquire@OMFLit.com
or call us at   531-6635
or text us: OMFLIT<space><TITLE OF BOOK>
                      <your comments> and send to 2299

If you have a blog, you may want to publish
a review of this book. Please let us know,
so we can read it too, and perhaps acknowledge
your review on our website.

www.OMFLit.com

OMF LITERATURE INC.
Publishing Truth.
Shaping Generations.
www.OMFLit.com

IT'S NOT ABOUT ME

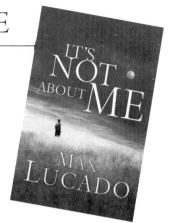

*Rescue from the Life
We Thought Would Make Us Happy*
BY MAX LUCADO

We've been demanding our way since day one . . . "I want a spouse that makes me happy and co-workers that always ask for my opinion." "I want weather that suits me and traffic that helps me and a government that serves me."

Self-promotion. Self-preservation. Self-centeredness . . .

"It's all about me."

They all told us it was, didn't they? And we took them up on it. We thought self-celebration would make us happy . . .

But believing that has created chaos—noisy homes, stress-filled businesses, cutthroat relationships. We've chased so many skinny rabbits, says Max Lucado, that we've missed the fat one: the God-centered life.

If you want to shift into high gear with purpose, this is it: Life makes sense when we accept our place! Our pleasures, our problems, our gifts and talents . . . when they're all for the One who created us, we suddenly gain what we've been missing and find what we've been seeking.

Let Max Lucado show you how to make the shift of a lifetime. How to bump your life off self-center. How to be changed and experience the meaning-charged life you were meant to have. Your discovery starts here.

Pick up a copy at your favorite bookstore!

GOD IS THERE IN THE TOUGH TIMES

Turning Your Disappointments into Hope

BY ED HINDSON

Even in life's worst moments, God is always nearer to us than we will ever know. No problem is beyond His ability to handle. As we draw upon the solutions the Lord gives in the Bible, we can turn our weaknesses into strengths, our disappointments into hope.

In this book, you will learn how to . . .

- Face crisis with confidence
- Find clear direction in the midst of confusion
- Turn a problem into an opportunity
- Conquer depression, stress, and feelings of failure
- Set realistic goals for change

Discover the biblical principles that can give you a whole new outlook on life's disappointments and hurts. Let God give you renewed hope today!

(Includes a Bible reference guide with answers to key problems people face)

Pick up a copy at your favorite bookstore!

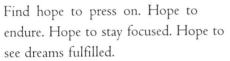

Hope Again

When Life Hurts and Dreams Fade
BY CHARLES SWINDOLL

Find hope to press on. Hope to endure. Hope to stay focused. Hope to see dreams fulfilled.

Combining the New Testament teachings of the apostle Peter and the insights of one of the most popular authors of our day, *Hope Again* is an encouraging, enlivening, and refreshing look at why we can dare to hope no matter who we are, no matter what we face.

As Charles Swindoll says, "If you want to smile through your tears, if you want to rejoice through times of suffering, just keep reminding yourself that what you're going through isn't the end of the story . . . it's simply the tough journey that leads to the right destination."

Pick up a copy at your favorite bookstore!

13/1.5K/6.2013/RT